D1461687

ECONOMIC CONTROVERSIES

Innovative and thought-provoking, the Economic Controversies series strips back the often impenetrable facade of economic jargon to present bold new ways of looking at pressing issues, while explaining the hidden mechanics behind them. Concise and accessible, the books bring a fresh, unorthodox approach to a variety of controversial subjects.

Also available in the Economic Controversies series:

Robert R. Locke and J.-C. Spender, *Confronting Managerialism: How the Business Elite and Their Schools Threw Our Lives Out of Balance*

Heikki Patomäki, *The Great Eurozone Disaster: From Crisis to Global New Deal*

Yanis Varoufakis, *The Global Minotaur: America, Europe and the Future of the Global Economy*

ABOUT THE AUTHOR

LORENZO FIORAMONTI is Jean Monnet Chair in Regional Integration and Governance Studies and Associate Professor of Political Science at the University of Pretoria (South Africa), where he directs the Centre for the Study of Governance Innovation. He is also Senior Fellow at the Centre for Social Investment of the University of Heidelberg and at the Hertie School of Governance (Germany) as well as Associate Fellow at the United Nations University. He is the author of numerous books and articles about development policies, alternative economies and social progress indicators and the director of a short film documentary on GDP and climate change, which can be viewed at his blog, www. globalreboot.org.

GROSS DOMESTIC PROBLEM

The politics behind the world's
most powerful number

LORENZO FIORAMONTI

Zed Books
LONDON | NEW YORK

To my wife, Janine, and my son, Damiano,
who make my life worthwhile

339.31

Gross Domestic Problem: The Politics behind the World's Most Powerful Number was first published in 2013 by Zed Books Ltd, 7 Cynthia Street, London N1 9JF, UK

Second impression, 2013

www.zedbooks.co.uk

Designed and typeset in Monotype Bulmer
by illuminati, Grosmont
Index: John Barker
Cover design by www.reactor15.com

A catalogue record for this book is available from the British Library
Library of Congress Cataloging in Publication Data available

ISBN 978 1 78032 273 5 hb
ISBN 978 1 78032 272 8 pb

Contents

Acknowledgements

The idea for this book came a few years ago, when I was invited by the Italian National Institute of Statistics (ISTAT) to participate in a meeting on alternative measures to the gross domestic product (GDP). It was a gathering of esteemed progressive economists and statisticians, which laid the groundwork for a fruitful partnership with civil society groups that continues to this day. As the only political scientist involved in the proceedings, I immediately realized that something was missing. While the discussion was all focused on how to improve statistical research, I felt that some analysis of the history and politics of GDP was also necessary to understand this number's powerful grip on our societies. So my first thanks go to ISTAT for inviting me, especially Tommaso Rondinella and the institute's president Enrico Giovannini, who have dedicated their careers to rethinking GDP.

The research that went into this book would not have been possible without the support of the Centre for Social Investment (CSI) at the University of Heidelberg, Germany. They offered me a generous fellowship, supported through a donation of the Compagnia di San Paolo, to conduct research on 'whatever subject' I fancied. This fellowship was a real luxury, especially in today's world, where academic freedom is ever more influenced by top-down imposed priorities and trapped into tight schedules of productivity. My gratitude, then, goes to the CSI management and, especially, to Georg Mildenberger for reading and commenting on each and every page of the manuscript.

As always, I owe an intellectual debt to a long list of people, which – no matter how crowded – could never be exhaustive. Among these I wish to mention Mario Pianta of the University of Urbino, Italy, who is also one of the promoters of the alternative economy web forum Sbilanciamoni.info; Helmut K. Anheier, who is the dean of the Hertie School of Governance, Berlin, Germany; and my South African colleagues, in particular Maxi Schoeman, Mzukisi Qobo and Prince Mashele of the University of Pretoria. Moreover, I would like to thank my editor, Ken Barlow, and the whole team at Zed Books for their support and magnificent assistance.

I completed the manuscript while sitting in my home office in Berlin, where I lived with my wife and son for most of 2012. It was the perfect location to work on a book about GDP, as the German capital provides a wealth of cultural resources amid an extremely laid-back atmosphere. Despite the inevitable aberrations of any urban settlement, the proximity of nature and the abundance of public spaces, playgrounds and other areas for leisure free of charge make Berlin one of the few 'big cities' in the world where some type of alternative life is still possible.

Lorenzo Fioramonti
Berlin, October 2012

The world's most powerful number

We are stealing the future, selling it in the present, and calling it GDP.

Paul Hawken

What we measure affects what we do; and if our measurements are flawed, decisions may be distorted.

Commission on the Measurement of
Economic Performance and Social Progress

Roughly eighty years after the Great Depression of the 1930s, the world has known another catastrophic financial and economic collapse. The Great Recession that began in 2008 has by no means been the only crisis that globalized capitalism has known in the past few years. Yet it has been the largest in scale. Exports have plummeted, jobs have been lost throughout the world and investment has fallen. Home foreclosures have become a daily routine, especially in the United States and in Southern Europe, where personal and public debt has reached unprecedented levels. Even an economic giant such as the European Union (the largest market on earth) has been taken on a financial roller coaster, spurring divisions among member states and rehashing old resentments across European peoples.

Over the past decades, not only social and economic inequalities but also the planet's natural resources have been depleted at a pace that, for the first time in history, has raised concerns among environmental groups and policymakers alike. Climate change, the epitome of all environmental degradation problems, has become part and parcel of the public debate the world over. According to the UN-sponsored Intergovernmental Panel on Climate Change, the emissions of greenhouse gases in the atmosphere due to human activities have vertiginously multiplied since the Industrial Revolution, and in particular since the mid-1900s. Unless major precautions are taken, the Panel forecasts serious risks for the global climate, with disastrous repercussions on those ecosystems that make biological and human life possible.[1]

Although media attention is almost exclusively focused on the world's treacherous 'road to economic recovery', the turmoil triggered by the economic crisis and the preoccupations with climate degradation seem to suggest that a business-as-usual solution to the world's problems is no longer feasible. As part of this process, an important – albeit still marginal – debate on the sustainability of the current economic system based on infinite economic growth has commenced. Such a critique is not only focusing on the inherent instability of market dynamics, but also on the more long-term impact that growth processes exert on the planet's limited natural resources and societal well-being at large. Does our quality of life improve when the economy grows by 2 or 3 per cent? Can we sacrifice our ecosystems to safeguard an economic framework marred by internal inconsistencies and imbalances? For the first time, the gross domestic product, which is the popular icon of economic growth, is being called into question. Even a defender of economic conservatism such as *The Economist* hosted an online debate on the issue in 2010 and concluded that 'GDP is a poor measure of improving living standards.'[2] The Organisation for Economic Co-operation and

Development (OECD), another bastion of economic traditionalism, has also been casting doubts on the dogma of GDP growth. It recognizes that

> for a good portion of the 20th century there was an implicit assumption that economic growth was synonymous with progress: an assumption that a growing GDP meant life must be getting better. But now the world recognizes that it isn't quite as simple as that. Despite high levels of economic growth in many countries, we are no more satisfied with our life (or happier) than we were 50 years ago [and] increased income has come at the expense of increased insecurity, longer working hours and greater complexity in our lives.[3]

For decades, the GDP mantra has dominated public debate and the media. Countries are ranked according to GDP, the global definition of 'power' is based on GDP (e.g. superpowers, emerging powers, etc.), access to global governance institutions is also granted on GDP performance (e.g. the G8 or G20 members are selected according to their GDP) and development policies are driven by the GDP formula. Currently, governments striving to come of out of the Great Recession largely design their policies and strategic choices following the diktat of GDP growth, and even global efforts to curb climate change and greenhouse gas emissions are being opposed by many countries because they may exert a negative impact on global GDP growth.

This book traces the history of GDP, discusses how its formula was developed and why it became so popular. In doing so, it analyses the key political and economic interests supporting GDP and the type of society it contributed to building. It also provides the first comprehensive review of the most important criticisms against GDP and the alternatives developed by experts, activists and civil society movements. From a political perspective, the current critique of GDP is becoming a catalyst for people's struggle to rethink our society and fight its long-standing inequalities and injustices.

What is GDP?

The measurement of wealth has a long tradition in modern economic thought. In the 1600s, the British political economist William Petty conducted the first ever survey of national wealth by systematically analysing the value of the land conquered by Oliver Cromwell in Ireland. Throughout the years, Petty tried to devise a host of mathematical formulae to measure not only the value of property but also that of labour, with a view to creating an account system that could be of service to government (especially for taxation purposes) while strengthening economic growth in modern Britain. For many reasons, including his sophisticated conceptualization and methodology, he was far ahead of his time. Back then, indeed, mainstream political economy was largely influenced by mercantilism, which considered the overall endowment owned by the king as the best indicator of a country's wealth. Based on this principle, Jean Baptiste Colbert, the powerful finance minister under French King Louis XIV, designed a strong top-down (*dirigiste*) institutional structure to ensure that commerce would serve French interests at the expense of neighbouring countries, thus producing an accumulation of gold in the national reserves and a positive balance of trade. During roughly the same period, his view was challenged by the Physiocrats, a group of (mainly French) economists who believed that the wealth of a nation was derived exclusively from the value of land, including its agricultural potential and development. They divided society into the proprietary class, made up of landowners; the productive class, which consisted of agricultural labourers; and the sterile class, which included artisans, professionals, merchants and, lo and behold, the king himself. Firm believers in private property and the emancipation of the bourgeoisie, the Physiocrats equated the economic output of a country with the productive work of agriculture and viewed the production of goods and services as consumption of the agricultural surplus.

The view that society is divided between productive and unproductive functions influenced most modern political economy. For instance, according to the father of classical economics, Adam Smith, the wealth of nations is generated by the productive labour of individuals. All other functions and services, no matter how prestigious they are made out to be, do not possess any intrinsic economic value:

> The labour of some of the most respectable orders in the society is, like that of menial servants, unproductive of any value …
> The sovereign, for example, with all the officers both of justice and war who serve under him, the whole army and navy, are unproductive labourers. They are the servants of the public, and are maintained by a part of the annual produce of the industry of other people.[4]

Yet Smith did not limit the wealth of a nation to land. Building on an argument previously put forward by Petty, he argued that a country's income is generated by 'the whole annual produce of the land and labour'. In his magnum opus, *The Wealth of Nations*, he maintained that this income is 'ultimately destined for supplying the consumption of its inhabitants':

> yet when it first comes either from the ground, or from the hands of the productive labourers, it naturally divides itself into two parts. One of them, and frequently the largest, is, in the first place, destined for replacing a capital, or for renewing the provisions, materials, and finished work, which had been withdrawn from a capital; the other for constituting a revenue either to the owner of this capital, as the profit of his stock, or to some other person, as the rent of his land.[5]

Similarly, for another classical political economist such as David Ricardo the value of a good is proportional not only to how much labour is necessary to produce it, but also to the labour required to manufacture the raw materials and machinery used in the process. And for Karl Marx all members of society 'can obtain their share of the annual product of commodities ... primarily only out of the hands of those classes who are the first to handle the product, that is to say, productive laborers, industrial capitalists, and real estate owners'.[6]

In contemporary societies, the wealth of a nation is usually measured in terms of GDP and expressed not in long and tedious paragraphs of ink – as was the case for classical economics – but in a single number, which every three months tells us how fast or slowly a country's economy is growing. In the US, the Bureau of Economic Analysis at the Department of Commerce is in charge of the national income and product accounts, while in most other countries national income estimates are usually published by statistical offices.

GDP measures the value of goods and services produced in a given time period, generally every three months. It measures production output in terms of market prices and can be represented by the following formula:

GDP = consumption + investment + government spending
      + exports – imports

The economist Simon Kuznets was responsible for the creation of the first national accounts in the US. In a report presented to Congress in 1934, Kuznets provided a first general definition of GDP, which is worth reporting in its entirety:

> Year in, year out the people of this country, assisted by the stock of goods in their possession, render a vast volume of services towards the satisfaction of their wants. Each of these services involves an effort on the part of an individual and an expenditure of some portion of the country's stock of goods. Some of these services eventuate in commodities, such as coal, steel,

clothing, furniture, automobiles; others take the form of direct, personal services, such as are rendered by physicians, lawyers, government officials, domestic servants, and the like. If all the commodities produced and all the direct services rendered during the year are added at their market value, and from the resulting total we subtract the value of that part of the nation's stock of goods that was expended (both as raw materials and as capital equipment) in producing this total, then the remainder constitutes the net product of the national economy during the year. It is referred to as national income produced, and may be defined briefly as that part of the economy's end product that results from the efforts of the individuals who comprise a nation.[7]

As explained by Kuznets himself, GDP 'may be represented as a cross-section at any stage in the circulation of economic goods – production, distribution or consumption – with results that, if no statistical difficulties are met, should be identical'.[8] As a consequence, there are three ways to measure it. First, GDP can be measured as the sum of all expenditures (or purchases) made by final users. This is known as the 'expenditures approach' and data is collected from companies, service-sector firms, retailers, government departments and the like. Given that the market price of a final good or service *should* reflect all incomes earned and costs incurred in the production process, GDP can also be measured as the sum of these charges. This is known as the 'income approach' (or gross domestic income) and is often used to assess the purchasing power of households and the financial health of business. In addition, GDP can also be measured as the sum of the value added at each stage of the production process. The 'value-added approach' to measuring GDP, which is carried out through specific surveys of thousands of firms (especially in the manufacturing and service sectors), allows the dissecting of national income by type of industry and is generally used to examine the composition of industrial outputs.[9]

GDP is designed to capture the quantity of production in a given time period, regardless of whether that production is used for immediate consumption, for investment in new fixed assets or inventories, or for replacing depreciated fixed assets. But in the production process, assets and capital are also consumed due to ageing, wear and tear, accidental damage and obsolescence. When this 'economic' depreciation is subtracted from GDP, the result is the 'net' domestic product – that is, an estimate of how much of a country's output is de facto available for real consumption, which means how many goods and services are actually provided to consumers. The net product is evidently a more accurate measure of production (as it excludes the investment that is necessary to replace consumed fixed assets), but calculation of depreciation is a lengthy and often cumbersome process. This has made its 'gross' cousin, GDP, the popular icon: its estimation is quicker and can be fed to the markets (and the media) on a quarterly basis.

For most of the twentieth century, national income was measured in terms of gross national product (GNP), which indicates the value of good and services produced by the residents of a country, regardless of whether the production takes place at home or abroad. The acronym GDP was introduced much later, in the early 1990s, when economic and financial globalization allowed companies to build subsidiaries across the world and delocalize. Due to its 'domestic' focus, GDP only measures the goods and services produced in-country, regardless of whether they are produced by national or foreign companies. As a consequence, an American company based in Shanghai counts towards China's GDP (and, conversely, America's GNP), while a Chinese firm based in Seattle adds to America's GDP (and, conversely, to China's GNP).[10] For simplicity's sake, this book will lump together historical/technical distinctions and, unless stated otherwise, will always refer to GDP.

The politics of GDP

There is no doubt that GDP is the best-known 'number' in the contemporary world and an extremely powerful political tool. Over the course of the past century, it has dominated not only in capitalist countries but also in socialist societies. And during the Cold War the GDP competition epitomized the profound rivalry between the two 'blocs' just as much as the arms race.

This magical number was invented in the 1930s to help America come out of the Great Depression. The then president, the Republican Herbert Hoover, was elected on the basis of a laissez-faire platform in economic policy, largely supported by the positive economic trends of the past decade, and his initial policies to curb the crisis proved dangerously ineffective. After only eight months in office, he had been catapulted into a devastating economic downturn, epitomized by the Black Tuesday of October 1929, when the US stock markets crashed, activating a domino effect throughout the world. The president was deeply convinced that markets would find their way out of the downturn without any direct intervention by government, but when the crisis worsened he tried to rely on more hands-on corrective policies, which needed some type of benchmark against which to gauge their capacity to stimulate a recovery. He scrambled for statisticians to help, but his government had no reliable and consistent measure of the state of the economy. When the Democrat Franklin D. Roosevelt won a landslide victory in 1932, the need for a methodology to measure national income became even more pressing. The whole New Deal philosophy, with its interventionist approach to macroeconomic stability, rested on the assumption that government was able to monitor closely the state of the economy and regularly assess the impact of its policies.

It was during these turbulent years that the first, primordial calculations of GDP were developed and the system of national

accounts created. A few years later, the Second World War, with
its massive need for a top-down command over economic production, sealed the close relationship between GDP and politics.
Indeed, the availability of regular and detailed statistics on the
strengths and weaknesses of industrial production helped the
American government outpace its enemies in terms of munitions
production. More importantly, it allowed for the conversion of
the civilian economy into a war machine without hampering
internal consumption, which turned out to be a major advantage
in generating revenues for the war (thus avoiding bottlenecks such
as those experienced by Hitler's war economy) and propelling
large-scale consumption in the post-war period. But GDP was
not just a number, it was also a powerful propaganda tool. This
is why, in the second half of the 1900s, the measurement of
economic performance became an important component of the
bipolar rivalry between the US and the Soviet Union, leading
to a proxy war involving secret services and economic experts,
which only ended with the fall of Communism.

In spite of its apparent neutrality, GDP has come to represent
a model of society, thereby influencing not only economic but
also political and cultural processes. GDP drives macroeconomic
governmental policies and sets priorities in the social fields. For
instance, according to the Stability and Growth Pact of the
European Union, the amount of funding that governments can
devote to public goods such as schooling and health care is generally 'tied' to GDP growth, resulting in a straightforward albeit
macabre equation: less GDP, less social investment. Moral principles such as equity, social justice and redistribution are subjected
to GDP calculations and are only taken up by policymakers if
they comply with the GDP-led development model. The so-called
Bush tax cuts, the largest in the recent history of America, were
amply justified by the need to foster GDP growth, while efforts
to secure increases in the federal living wage have been thwarted

by persistent gloom-and-doom forecasts with respect to overall GDP performance.[11] Our geography (from urbanization processes to the management of public/private areas) is dominated by the politics of GDP. Marketing strategies, advertising, consumption patterns and lifestyles are permeated by its influence. Even charity is dependent on GDP, as public and private philanthropy are generally correlated to the performance of economic growth: the more money is generated by the economy, the more funding is made available to 'do good'.

The rhetoric of GDP and its consumption model was also triumphant in political discourse. In no circumstance was this so clearly evident as in the first reactions of world leaders and opinion-makers to the terrorist attacks of 11 September 2001. Famously, US president George W. Bush urged Americans to 'get on the airlines, get about the business of America', and his British counterpart, Tony Blair, encouraged his compatriots 'to travel and to shop' in order to get the economy back on its feet.[12] Similarly, the then prime minister of Canada, Jean Chrétien, asserted that the best way to defeat terrorism was through sustained consumption: 'it is time to go out and get a mortgage, to buy a home, to buy a car.... The economy of the world needs people to go back to their lives.... It is the way to fight back.'[13] In a radio interview ten days after the attacks, New York's mayor Rudy Giuliani put it quite clearly: 'There is a way that everybody can help us, New Yorkers and everybody all over the country. Come here and spend money ... And go shopping, we're the best shoppers in the world.'[14] Republicans and Democrats, conservatives and progressives, parliamentarians and local administrators were all united by the same creed. Thousands of letters flooded American newspapers with encouragements for people to go back to their usual consumption habits. 'The patriotic thing to do is: hold your stocks and buy more; get on an airplane and get on with doing business; start shopping again', said a letter to the

Miami Herald the week after the attacks. 'America, you love to shop, so get going.'[15]

Being presented as an essential tool for the design of public policies, the invention of GDP also afforded unprecedented power to technocrats and business specialists. Politicians could no longer do their jobs without the continuous support of economic advisers. Academic economists left classrooms and began successful (and hugely remunerated) political careers, while many faculties of economics ceased to be arenas of free thinking to become instead assembly lines of economic consultants. As political economy was crystallized in the hands of specialists, its goals and objectives were taken away from daily political contestation. Society came to accept that those at the helm knew what was best for all. Individuals were disempowered as citizens and glorified as consumers.

Over the course of its life, GDP has shaped our understanding of economic progress. It has lauded the impact of industrial production (especially the heavy polluting industries) and undervalued that of technological innovation. Moreover, it has intentionally neglected the overall weight of the informal economy, from the innumerable services rendered at the household level to the many 'odd jobs' that provide the necessary subsistence to millions of people and often constitute the backbone of the real economy. Yet, as reported by the IMF, the informal economy has reached remarkable levels worldwide: in 2002, it accounted for up to 44 per cent of output in developing nations, 30 per cent in transition economies, and 16 per cent in the OECD countries.[16]

GDP stylized social complexity into dry numbers and, in doing so, it perpetrated market society at the expenses of human, social and ecological concerns. It ushered in an era of material wealth (at least for some people in industrialized societies) while generating inequalities, depletion of natural resources and growing social distress.

GDP and its critics

The notion that economic growth produces not only goods but also 'bads' (that is, negative externalities) has been part and parcel of modern capitalism since its origins. Yet, during the early onset of the market economy in the eighteenth century, intellectuals and opinion leaders viewed the collateral effects of expanding commerce and industrial production as largely positive. For instance, the theory of *doux commerce* (gentle commerce) heralded by Montesquieu depicted capitalism as a gentle force 'which polishes and softens barbaric ways'. In his *View of the Progress of Society in Europe* (1769), a major account of European history from the collapse of the Roman Empire to the modern age, the Scottish historian William Robertson fully endorsed Montesquieu's appreciation for the growth of commerce, and one of his contemporaries, the French philosopher and mathematician Condorcet, maintained that manners had become 'more gentle through the influence of the spirit of commerce and industry'. Similarly, in the words of one of the intellectual masterminds of both the American and the French Revolution, Thomas Paine, commerce 'is a pacific system, operating to cordialise mankind, by rendering Nations, as well as individuals, useful to each other'.[17]

However, most of this early optimism was soon dispelled by the impact that the Industrial Revolution had on social relations. The economic historian Arnold Toynbee argued that the first half of the nineteenth century was 'a period as disastrous and as terrible as any through which a nation has ever passed'. It was disastrous and terrible because, side by side with a great increase in wealth was seen an enormous increase in pauperism; and production on a vast scale, the result of free competition, led to a rapid alienation of classes and the degradation of a large body of producers.[18]

Looking at the social consequences of economic growth in the Victorian era, the English writer Thomas Carlyle famously labelled economics 'the dismal science'. 'Supply-and-demand, Leave-it-alone, Voluntary Principle, Time will mend it', he wrote in 1850. 'Till British industrial existence seems fast becoming one huge poison-swamp of reeking pestilence physical and moral.'[19] In the *Communist Manifesto* and other early writings, Marx and Engels described how capitalist relations eroded traditional values and institutions such as love, family and patriotism by annihilating the value of anything that could not be immediately monetized. Charles Dickens wrote his hugely successful *A Christmas Carol* as an attack on modern business and its lack of humanity and sympathy.

Over the past decades, progressive economists, ecologically minded think-tanks and NGOs have been criticizing GDP with a view to limiting its influence on policymaking. A myriad alternative indicators have been produced in an effort to dethrone this 'almighty number' and produce more reliable measures of societal well-being. Indicators comparing economic performance and environmental resources have also been available for quite some time, inspired by theories of 'genuine progress', stressing the need to account for the human and environmental costs of economic growth. Yet, until now, this critique has been limited to a small circle of experts, while GDP has continued growing in popularity and influence. Only recently, the convergence of the environmental and economic 'crises' has brought new blood into this debate, also triggering important actions within the political arena.

Some of these actions are only cosmetic (characterized by some 'greenwashing' elements) while others aim at more radical changes. For instance, in 2004 China announced that a 'green' GDP would become the country's main economic indicator in order to account for the financial impact of environmental degradation, pollution and other negative externalities. In November 2007 the EU hosted a high-level conference titled 'Beyond GDP' and, two years later, the Commission released a communication on 'GDP and Beyond: Measuring Progress in a Changing World', where it argued that GDP has been unduly 'regarded as a proxy indicator for overall societal development and progress in general'. But, since it does not measure environmental sustainability or social inclusion, 'its limitations need to be taken into account when using it in policy analysis and debates'.[20] The special commission on social progress set up by former French president Nicolas Sarkozy and chaired by Nobel laureates Joseph Stiglitz and Amartya Sen also highlighted the profound inadequacy of GDP as a measure of well-being. Its 2009 report identified a number of alternative indicators to replace GDP and reminded us that GDP is a measure of market production, though it has often been treated as if it were a measure of economic well-being: 'Conflating the two can lead to misleading indications about how well-off people are and entail the wrong policy decisions.'[21]

Many economists have questioned GDP. Some of them have focused on its internal inconsistencies, others have pointed out its shortcomings as a measure of welfare, while others – the most radical – have rejected the very idea of economic growth, arguing it is incompatible with the finite resources of our planet. Due to the variety of arguments, the present book cannot do justice to each and every GDP critic. A dozen volumes would be necessary to dissect each thesis in detail and discuss the piles of paper that have been written against GDP. Thus, for the sake of space and narrative thread, only the most significant critiques will be mentioned in the rest of the book.

Most importantly, though, GDP growth has been criticized not only by experts, but also by ordinary people. This has been particularly true in industrialized societies, where the GDP creed was first developed before being 'sold' to the rest of the world. These days, North America and Europe are in the eye of the storm, ravaged by international speculators and apparently unable to run the race of 'growth at all costs' against the formidable competition of China, India and a bunch of other fast-growing economies. Quite unexpectedly, this predicament has turned the 'old West' into a fertile terrain for revisionist approaches. New civil society initiatives and campaigns are being promoted throughout both continents with a view to fighting GDP and radically rethinking our dominant economic model. A variety of community associations, non-governmental organizations, environmental movements and other civil society groups have been experimenting with creative models, ranging from alternative currencies to 'degrowth' initiatives, in order to promote well-being, defend public goods and preserve our ecosystems.

CHAPTER 1

The history of GDP:
from crisis to crisis

While the GDP and the rest of the national income accounts may seem to be arcane concepts, they are truly among the great inventions of the twentieth century.

Paul A. Samuelson and William D. Nordhaus,
Nobel laureates in Economics

The invention of GDP was the 'Manhattan project' of economics.

Alan AtKisson, author of *The Sustainability Transformation*

Although the first attempts at measuring national income date back to seventeenth-century Ireland, the current systems of national accounts have a much more recent history. The gross domestic product, or gross national product as it was initially called, was invented in the twentieth century in a time of profound economic crisis. It was the Great Depression of the 1930s, with its heavy toll on industrial production and employment, that prompted policymakers and economists in the United States to join forces with a view to developing a systematic method to assess the state of the national economy and its performance over time. At that time, government needed more reliable evidence to guide its macroeconomic policies given that existing data was too sketchy and hard to compare. With the outbreak of the Second World War, the defence budget became the most significant propeller of America's economic output and large industries were to be quickly converted into producers of ammunition and military equipment. In this context, the capacity to estimate the speed at which the civilian economy could be effectively converted into a war machine without hampering internal consumption turned out to be one of the most critical advantages of the US vis-à-vis other countries, especially Nazi Germany. For all intents and purposes, the invention of GDP helped America win the war at least as much as the development of the nuclear bomb carried out by the Manhattan Project. No surprise, then, that such a close connection between GDP and the war economy continued unabated in the post-war period and especially with the end of the Cold War, when the US asserted itself as the only superpower and its model of consumption won the hearts and minds of most of the world.

Ever since, GDP has been dominating the policies of international financial institutions, such as the World Bank and the International Monetary Fund, and has driven virtually every sector of political and economic governance. In the past few decades, GDP performance has become the number one priority of most (if not all) countries around the world, irrespective of their political leadership, industrial development and cultural background. Until another crisis hit: the Great Recession starting in 2008, which converged with the environmental degradation caused by economic growth. This chapter tells the story of how all of this came about.

Numbers and politics: the pre-history of GDP

The first attempt at designing a system of national economic accounts was made in Ireland in 1652, when a physician of the

British army, William Petty, was asked to conduct a systematic survey of the country's wealth as part of a land redistribution programme promised by Cromwell to his troops in the aftermath of a repressed uprising. Within thirteen months, and with the help of innovative surveying instruments as well as trained soldiers, Petty completed the study and drew up maps of roughly thirty counties, which stretched for over 5 million acres. The Down Survey, as it is commonly known, represented the first ever attempt to measure the wealth of a country through systematic economic analysis. And, perhaps not surprisingly, its application soon revealed hidden political agendas. For starters, the survey was designed to serve the interests of the British government, whose main goal was to put its Irish problem to rest by expropriating the country's populace (especially its Catholic component) of productive land and turning it into a source of income for a permanent occupational presence. Some historians have demonstrated the extent to which this statistical undertaking helped eradicate Ireland's indigenous culture,[1] while others have described it as a 'gigantic experiment in primitive accumulation'.[2] Petty's work was also instrumental in equipping government with new information to raise taxes and limit the amount of wealth owned by private individuals, a useful piece of intelligence to restrain local autonomy and avoid concentrations of capital in the hands of potential opponents.

On a personal level, the survey also turned into a gold mine for Petty's financial assets. Only a few years later, this young son of an English clothier had acquired nearly 19,000 acres of Irish land, some of which was given to him in lieu of salary, and some of which he was able to purchase from the soldiers to whom the land had been granted by government. How did he manage this? Because, according to the law based on the results of his survey, most of this land was declared 'unprofitable' and thus it could be bought very cheaply. Yet, in spite of its alleged unprofitability, it constituted the primary source of Petty's considerable fortune: while in 1652 his total assets had been less than £500, in 1685 he could count on a personal wealth worth of over £6,700.[3] Although Parliament tried to impeach him on several occasions, charging that he had taken bribes and had profited unfairly from his official position, the government protected him, and when the monarchy was finally re-established in 1660 all charges against him were immediately dropped. King Charles II pardoned him for his service under Cromwell, awarded him a knighthood and, by royal letter, secured all his personal holdings in Ireland.

According to historian Mary Poovey, Petty forged the link 'between personal experience, mathematics, and impartiality that made his experience in Ireland seem both essential and incidental to the kind of knowledge he produced for the king':

> Numerical representation was critical to this link, because the credibility of numbers that purported simply to reflect what had been counted was enhanced by firsthand experience, while the precision of 'computing' seemed to efface the personal interest of the person who made knowledge from numbers.[4]

Petty's close relationship with government and, personally, with the king, allowed him to continue influencing Britain's economic policies. Among others, he recommended that the state keep records about domestic consumption, production, trade, and population growth as part of a centralization process that would eventually strengthen the government at the expense of peripheral pockets of autonomy. He also made the case that keeping track of domestic production would have improved the collection of taxes and the design of economic policies to support the expansion of Britain vis-à-vis competitors in Europe. In his *Economic Writings*, Petty argued that 'if every mans Estate could be alwayes read in his forehead', then economic activities would prosper and the nation's wealth would grow indefinitely.[5] Obviously, this type of accounting would require more than simply distinguishing

profitable from unprofitable land. Among others, it would need
some measurement of the value of each property, which would
inevitably include the amount of labour necessary to make it
profitable and sustain production. Thus, by venturing into the
complex world of economic accounting, Petty began to focus
on these issues during the latter part of his life as an economic
advisor to the Crown. His objective was to develop an 'impartial'
method to compare the value of property and labour in order to
make both subject to taxation. In his view, a more sophisticated
national account system would assure the sovereign that 'he would
eventually be able to collect the assessed taxes', thus making
government more inclined to let money circulate freely in society
and let the subjects trade and produce.[6] He envisioned society
as an economic collectivity whose overall production was in the
interest of Britain's projected power in the world. Even though
some individuals may experience losses and others may gain
out of this process, what really mattered to Petty was that the
nation, as an economic entity, could grow. What some saw as a
contest between the government and the people, he portrayed as
a common effort directed against other nations. And 'what could
look like a game of chance' became a circulation of wealth 'that
seemed equitable'.[7]

As part of his effort to 'modernize' the British political
economy, Petty did not limit himself to measuring quantifiable
entities. Having developed an interest for the economic assessment of the worth of labour, he believed that it was possible to
use statistical techniques to extrapolate 'the value of the people'.[8]
According to his approach, 'value' should be gauged exclusively
in monetary terms, without any other psychological, ethical or
religious connotation.

> Suppose the People of England be Six Millions in number, that
> their expence at 7l. per Head by forty two Millions: suppose
> also that the Rent of the Lands be eight Millions, and the profit

of all the Personal Estates be Eight Millions more; it must
needs follow, that the Labour of the People must have supplyed
the remaining Twenty Six Millions, the which multiplied
by Twenty (the Mass of Mankind being worth Twenty Years
purchase as well as Land) makes Five Hundred and Twenty
Millions, as the value of the whole People: which number
divided by Six Millions, makes above 8ol. Sterling, to be
valued of each Head of Man, Woman and Child, and of adult
Persons twice as much; from which we may learn to compute
the loss we have sustained by the Plague, by the Slaughter of
Men in War, and by the sending them abroad into the Service
of Foreign Princes.[9]

As cynical as it might sound, Petty honestly believed that
human beings could be given a monetary value. Although he
never argued for the commercialization of people, he opined that
individuals were an economic resource of the country and, as
such, their economic value needed to be assessed in some way.
A firm believer in the impartiality of arithmetic, he presented
his approach as a factual representation of the worth of a nation,
even though it was largely based on generalizations and value
judgements. By relying on apparently neutral numbers, Petty
could hide the fact that his theory was shaping the way in which
government would end up regarding the populace: instruments
and commodities rather than human beings. Thus, soon after
Petty's time, preoccupations with economic performance took
priority over other objectives of public policymaking. And the
adoption of economic accounts to measure not just the income of
a nation but also the overall worth of a people would turn into a
powerful tool for the central government. Perhaps surreptitiously,
Petty's economic theory paved the way for the introduction of
cost–benefit analyses in policy planning. So, if the worth of a
human life could be monetized, then the king could easily weigh
the expense of disease prevention, for example, against the cost
of an unaddressed plague, or the human capital to be invested

in a military campaign against the loss it would cause in terms of domestic consumption.[10]

Just as Hobbes's mechanical representation of political power inaugurated modern political thought, William Petty's quest for mathematical representations of national wealth provided the foundations of modern political economy.[11] His attempt to turn the value of social phenomena (as well as human beings) into numbers was presented as a genuine effort at advancing knowledge and impartiality. In fact, it served the interests of the ruling elite and was amply adopted as an instrument of domination. And this has been true for all measures of economic performance, from that time to the present.

GDP as a 'war machine'

Although the collection of statistics to describe national economies has a long tradition in the Western world (as the pioneering work of William Petty demonstrates), the invention of the System of National Accounts (SNA) and the measurement of GDP are relatively recent. The SNA was created in the US over the course of the 1930s to allow the American government to jump-start the economy out of the Great Depression and, more importantly, to maximize production in what was soon to become a wartime economy.

The first set of national accounts was prepared under the guidance of the American Russian economist Simon Kuznets and a small team of young researchers. Of Jewish origin, Kuznets was born in the Russian Empire in 1901 and spent his childhood under the Tzar's rule. As an adolescent he sympathized with moderate Menshevik movements inspired by a reformist approach to Marxist socialism, and as a consequence he opposed the radicalism of Leninist Bolsheviks. When, after the 1917 October Revolution, the nation fell into civil war, the family fled the country and, via Turkey, migrated to the US, where Simon continued his studies in economics and received a Ph.D. from Columbia University.[12] Although during his academic career Kuznets held a number of chairs at various American universities, from the University of Pennsylvania to the Johns Hopkins University and ultimately Harvard, his major contributions to economics were made during his long tenure as a senior researcher at the National Bureau of Economic Research (NBER), a think-tank founded in 1920 that was soon to become the leading economic research organization in the US. As one of the students and closest collaborators of the NBER's founding director, the renowned political economist Wesley C. Mitchell, who had been appointed chairman of President Hoover's Committee on Social Trends, Kuznets was immediately exposed to the various ranks of the US policy community of the time.

By the late 1920s, the Great Depression had hit America. Workers were being retrenched on a daily basis, capital markets were up in arms and entire industries were on the brink of collapse. Although the federal government tried to tackle the situation with the various means at its disposal, the absence of systematic and regular data on the state of the economy threatened the effectiveness of economic policies. According to economist Richard T. Froyen, 'One reads with dismay of Presidents Hoover and then Roosevelt designing policies to combat the Great Depression of the 1930s on the basis of such sketchy data as stock price indices, freight car loadings, and incomplete indices of industrial production.'[13] As America sank deeper into an economic slough, the White House called on the Department of Commerce to produce some factual evidence to assess whether the government's policies were actually working. President Hoover himself, having been a former secretary of commerce, was able to exert direct influence on the Department's bigwigs to come up with some numbers. Elections were looming and his job as the first citizen of America was on the line. Amid mounting political pressure, a handful of employees were dispatched throughout the country with a view to collecting data and filing reports about industrial production.[14] Their capacity was limited and their methods largely ad hoc; thus it came as no surprise that such anecdotal evidence tended to support Hoover's view that recovery was just around the corner. But, as it turned out, it was not.

Meanwhile, Kuznets had begun to work on the conceptualization and measurement of national income, and in 1932 he authored an article for the *Encyclopaedia of the Social Sciences*. An early draft of his entry landed on the desk of a Democratic senator from Wisconsin, Marion LaFollette, who convinced his fellow congressmen that the time had come to stop compiling sketchy reports aimed at assuaging the White House and invest in a more systematic and reliable methodology.[15] LaFollette wrote up a resolution that was immediately approved by the US Congress. The Department of Commerce was officially tasked with producing national income estimates for all years since the commencement of the Great Depression (1929–31) in order to gauge not just the current state of the economy but also its performance over time.[16] Due to the lack of scientific expertise, the Department turned to the NBER to provide technical assistance and the research project was entrusted to Kuznets. With the help of two other young economists, Milton Gilbert, who would then become the main author of the official figures published by the Department of Commerce, and Robert Nathan, who would later on enjoy a brilliant career as economic adviser to President Roosevelt, Kuznets was finally given the opportunity to put his theories to the test. In spite of the limited financial and human resources, he completed the estimates in record time.[17]

Kuznets's idea was very simple: generate a series of aggregate measures capable of condensing all economic production by individuals, companies and the government into a single number, which should rise in good times and fall in bad. The initial work by Kuznets spurred particular interest among American governmental officialdom and prompted the NBER to launch a series of annual conferences to forge closer links between academia and government. Up until that time, economists and policymakers had been living in two relatively separate worlds. But, with the compilation of national statistical accounts, the room for cooperation in policy design (especially in the field of macroeconomic policy) grew considerably. The first Conference on Research in Income and Wealth was organized in 1936 under the leadership of Kuznets and free-market economist Milton Friedman. Participants came from the Economics departments of six leading universities (Chicago, Columbia, Harvard, Minnesota, Pennsylvania and Wisconsin); the US Departments of Commerce (Bureau of Foreign and Domestic Commerce), Agriculture, Treasury, and Labor (Bureau of Labor Statistics); the National Resources Committee; the Board of Governors of the Federal Reserve System; the Central Statistical Board; the National Industrial Conference Board; and the National Bureau of Economic Research.[18] Academics, experts, regulators, policymakers and the key interest groups in the industrial sector were duly represented in the proceedings.

The conference focused not only on the results of the first assessments of national income and the current state of research in the field of capital formation, but also on some key methodological and conceptual issues, especially in so far as these could affect the design and implementation of macroeconomic policies. As Kuznets would recall later on, it was during this conference that the term 'gross national product', GNP, was first introduced as a macro-measure of economic output, while the definition of national income was restricted to the 'net' component of national product by subtracting the value of commodities (especially the depreciation of capital) consumed in the process of production.[19]

During the first three years of the conference series, there were significant disagreements among the participants, some of whom contested not only the key concepts underpinning the measurement, but also the 'content' of it. Heated debates were triggered, for example, by the division between those who would exclude capital gains and losses from the final computation and those who would include them. Divergent opinions surfaced also with regard to the evaluation of services rendered by government. Indeed, while the value of most commodities could be measured in terms of market prices, governmental services were likely to be influenced by political considerations and their price imposed by the state, thus potentially affecting the ultimate calculation. Furthermore, Kuznets himself disagreed with those endorsing a completely value-free conception of national income as he firmly defended the exclusion of the net value product of illegal enterprises from the total.[20]

Up until 1939, each annual conference published its proceedings in regular volumes made available to academics and experts. From 1940 onwards, though, the meetings began taking place behind closed doors and the publication of proceedings was suspended. While in 1940 the Bureau declared that the discussion were of 'insufficient general interest to warrant publication', in the following years it became evident that the focus of the conference shifted from the measurement of national income per se to the more pressing issue of how to use the national accounts to support America's effort in the Second World War.[21] Once again, the minutes were not published given that 'interest in the subject matter of some of the papers was restricted, and that some of the others were primarily of temporary ... concern'.[22]

There is little doubt that the NBER's work on national accounts profoundly influenced the second phase of the New Deal and contributed to strengthening the policy appeal of Keynesianism among American scholars and policymakers. Since Keynesian policies aimed to sustain economic performance through flows of money from government to society, a system of national accounts capable of producing regular data to assess the impact of national policies on the economy was essential to the government's planning. Therefore it is not surprising that one of John Maynard Keynes's disciples, Colin Clark, was responsible for developing the first set of economic accounts in Australia, and two British economists, Richard Stone and James Meade, largely influenced by Keynes's theories, were tasked with setting up the UK's national accounts in the early 1940s. The underlying philosophy was that, through proper fiscal management and taxation as well as detailed knowledge of economic performance (as indicated by GNP), economists and politicians could finally master the dreaded 'business cycle', which had caused continuous crises and job losses, and ensure prosperity indefinitely. The theoretical work of Keynes and the applied statistical method developed by Kuznets finally came together during the Second World War, when GNP was elevated to primary scorecard for the design and implementation of national economic policy.

In 1942, Kuznets went to work for the Planning Committee of the War Production Board, which was chaired by his former student and collaborator at the NBER, Robert Nathan. With the latter, Kuznets applied the national income approach to estimate the economy's productive capacity and locate areas of unused capacity that could be switched over to the munitions programme. Their calculations also provided a technical scaffolding to support the war capacity of the US economy through optimal readjustments, efficiency in military production and sustained civilian consumption.[23] Using national income and capital formation data, they were therefore able to stimulate an expansion of America's economic output by $17 million during the first twelve months of conflict. In just four years (1942–45), the share of material procurement in GNP rose from 4 per cent to 48 per cent, and in 1944, after the successful conversion of the automobile industry into an aircraft production chain, the US was producing twice as many war airplanes in a month as it had produced in the whole of 1939.[24]

In the early 1940s, before the US entered officially into war, a bitter debate had erupted in Washington among the heads of the various agencies set up by President Roosevelt to coordinate industrial policies. Some of them believed that the US could continue providing goods to its allies and ultimately take an active part in the Second World War without embarking on a major programme of reconversion of its civilian industry. According to them, there were vast resources that could be tapped into without militarizing existing industries. For others, the scale of the challenge and the likelihood of the direct military involvement of the US in the European battlefield made imposing a full conversion of the civilian industry while pushing for higher production targets inevitable.[25]

When President Roosevelt launched his Victory Program to turn America into a war machine and defeat the Axis forces led by Nazi Germany, the studies conducted by Kuznets and Nathan at the War Production Board helped identify equilibria between the objectives of military mobilization and the need to keep internal consumption growing, so as to generate additional long-term resources for the war efforts. Through a systematic estimation of national income and capital formation, already at the outset of US involvement in the war, Kuznets and Nathan were able to gauge how much of the material production called for by Roosevelt's Victory Plan could be achieved and when it would become available.[26] As reported by historian Jim Lacey in a book titled *How US Economists Won World War II*, these calculations 'also established that the United States was capable of a far greater effort than was currently being called for and that this could be accomplished without severely curtailing consumer consumption', which was by contrast essential to continue generating the necessary flow of resources sustaining national income.[27] These positions were also supported outside of the closed circles of the president's economic advisers and enjoyed a significant degree of popularity among those business leaders and corporations favouring the adoption of a series of national policies aimed at scaling up the military efforts while encouraging domestic consumption. In their opinion, this would have guaranteed windfall profits for their industries without forcing them into a full conversion programme or an outright (albeit temporary) nationalization. What they wanted was for industrial interests to define military priorities, not for the army to take over production facilities.

The data collection work and the statistical models prepared by Kuznets and colleagues also impacted on specific aspects of military planning. For instance, their estimates of GNP growth combined with those pertaining to the costs of the military campaign led them to conclude that the US government should avoid the direct involvement of armed forces in Europe until the end of 1943 or beginning of 1944. According to their calculations, production levels and munitions would have not sustained an earlier intervention onto the battlefield.

Their feasibility approach to the president's Victory Program was unavoidably met with resistance by the military apparatus and the 'all-outers', a group of political advisers to Roosevelt who argued for the country's quick and massive involvement in the war through seizing industries and private corporations. In their view, politics should have dominated the game, not economics: 'the strategists decide what their requirements are, and our job is to get industry to fill those requirements.'[28] Confronted with long lists of numbers and theoretical estimates of abstract concepts such as 'national product in wartime', they plainly could not fathom how their 'high' targets could actually end up lowering the capacity of the economy to support the military effort and ultimately undermine the US's ability to win the war.

In the end, the economists prevailed and the government revised its approach to the munitions programme in order to follow the estimates provided by Kuznets and Nathan. As expected, the US economy boomed and the country's capacity to sustain military exposure appeared almost unlimited. Real consumption in the US rose sharply in 1941 and, after a slight drop in 1942, it rose again in 1943. By 1944, the US could afford to wage the war simultaneously on two fronts (Europe and the Pacific) while domestic personal civilian consumption was at an all-time high. To their great surprise, American investigators learned after the war that Hitler's military production targets were unrealistically disconnected from the overall performance of the German economy, a deficiency arguably caused by the lack of sophisticated systems of national accounts.[29]

According to Kuznets's former boss and founding director of the NBER, Wesley C. Mitchell, 'Only those who had a personal share in the economic mobilization for World War I could realize in how many ways and how much estimates of national income covering 20 years and classified in several ways facilitated the World War II effort.'[30] In the words of analysts Clifford Colb, Ted Halstead and Jonathan Rowe, 'the degree to which the GNP evolved as a war-planning tool is hard to exaggerate':

> In the United States the Manhattan Project got much more glory. But as a technical achievement the development of the GNP accounts was no less important. The accounts enabled the nation to locate unused capacity, and to exceed by far the production levels that conventional opinion thought possible.[31]

Overall, GNP accounts turned out to be a powerful instrument to estimate militarization costs and calculate what speed of economic growth would be necessary 'to pay for the war', to paraphrase a well-known paper written by Keynes in 1940 during his tenure at the British Treasury. Thanks to this systematic approach, America managed to come very close to pure economic planning, and in 1944 war production goals alone surpassed the nation's entire output just ten years earlier.[32] According to economist John Kenneth Galbraith, celebrated author of *The Affluent Society* and adviser to US president Kennedy, Kuznets and his talented colleagues had been the equivalent of several infantry divisions in their contribution to the American war effort.[33] Importantly, their work had a fundamental impact on the post-war recovery too. Based on their recommendations, the US government sustained internal consumption throughout the war without endangering civilian industries, which made it possible to collect additional resources for the mobilization effort while limiting the generation of an excess capacity that may have caused a new recession after the end of the war. As a consequence, by the end of the conflict Americans were left with a stronger industrial sector and a huge saving pool, which, coupled with pent-up consumer demand for durable consumer items, were the key factors propelling America's post-war economic expansion.

In 1946, Milton Gilbert, one of Kuznets's closest collaborators, who by then was in charge of the GNP computation at the Department of Commerce, recognized that 'war conditions and problems stimulated interest in analyzing the national economy of the United States and also in the national incomes of foreign countries involved in the war.'[34] Thus, in the early 1950s, GNP became the dominant metric of economic performance across the Western world, and in 1953 the United Nations inaugurated its international standards for national accounts, which were largely influenced by the methodology developed by Kuznets and the US Department of Commerce.

As the war was winding down, the accounts served to guide the economy back to peacetime without the risk of a relapse into economic stagnation. In order to guarantee continuous GNP growth, the government kept on incentivizing private consumption on a massive scale. Moreover, it increased its defence budget, which had the indirect consequence of strengthening the political and economic power of the so-called military–industrial complex, a web of business interests against whose growing influence in American politics President Eisenhower would later on warn his fellow citizens. During these years, the linkage between domestic consumerism and external military projection was so deeply integrated into economic design as to become a key feature of the US model of capitalism, thus replicating – although at varying degrees – the successful model that emerged out of the war.

Kuznets did not like these developments. Although he recognized that 'success in war and preservation of a country's social framework' may be considered 'at least equal in importance to the welfare of individuals', he nevertheless emphasized that one should 'beware of extending this view-point, justified by the necessarily temporary crises in the life of a nation, to the common run of public activities'.[35] Yet, with the breakout of the Cold War, most politicians and their economic advisers endorsed a view of economic growth opposite to that of Kuznets. They pushed for military expenditures to become a pillar of GNP expansion, a choice that its creator only considered legitimate during a war for national survival.[36] So, although Kuznets would continue arguing for a 'peacetime concept' of national income, the very success of GNP as a 'war machine' limited the capacity of political elites and opinion makers to realize the shortcomings that this number suffered from as an indicator of national welfare.

Manipulation and the 'stats war'

Although GNP had become the most popular measure of economic performance, its use was mostly limited to advanced capitalist economies and their allies. The rest of the world was a territory of conquest for statisticians and economists. Kuznets himself, for instance, helped the first Chinese government led by Chiang Kai-shek develop a system of national accounts based on the US experience in an effort to align China's economic policies with those of Western capitalism and oppose the diffusion of communism in East Asia.[37]

While most developing countries had no capacity to measure economic activities on a national scale, the nations comprising the socialist bloc used different metrics. Their system of calculation was based on two main indicators: the gross social product, which measured the total gross output of industries, and the net material product, which deducted from the former the material consumption generated by the industries in the production process.[38] According to the *Great Soviet Encyclopaedia*, the socialist society 'is able to produce and distribute the gross social product in accordance with the volume and structure of social needs on the basis of a unified national economic plan', while under the conditions of capitalist society the GNP has 'an antagonistic class character, since it is a physical expression of capitalist productive relations'.[39]

Following Marx's approach, the Soviet concept of national income was commonly defined as 'that part of the social product, evaluated in monetary terms, which is newly created each year by the labor of the society and becomes available annually for consumption and accumulation'.[40] This measurement only included physical goods, hence material product, and excluded all governmental and private services, which were – by contrast – an important component of Kuznets's calculation of national income. According to the socialist approach, services (whether public or private) did not constitute 'primary' or 'original' income but were merely the result of its distribution. Evidently, the Soviet concept of national income was much narrower than that of capitalist countries as it excluded, among other things, the government sector (generally measured by the salaries of employees in conventional GNP statistics) and the service industry.

The estimation of material product in the USSR was carried out by the Central Statistical Office (also known as Goskomstat), whose first calculations dated back to the early 1920s and, to all intents and purposes, could be considered a forerunner of Kuznets's SNA.[41] All socialist countries followed this approach (also known as the System of Balances of the National Economy) until the fall of the Soviet Union, the only exception being Hungary, which, in 1968, adopted a dual method of measuring national income in terms of both GNP and material product. For most of the interwar period, Soviet authorities published only aggregate totals of their national income. For international political and military reasons, they clamped down severely on the disclosure of any statistics on domestic economic operations.[42] After the end of the Second World War, USSR economists and policymakers became well aware of the differences between their methods and the GNP calculations, but instead of raising their own figures by including the missing items (e.g. services), they systematically lowered the GNP estimates of the US and the other capitalist societies by deducting the value of governmental and other services. This led them to conclude that, under socialism, the production of the gross social product had proceeded at an amazingly rapid rate. According to their official records, between 1928 and 1940, when the capitalist world was still grappling with the Great Depression, the size of gross social product had increased by a factor of 4.5, and from 1940 to 1969 by a factor of 7.5. By contrast, they estimated that in the US the GNP had only doubled between 1950 and 1968.[43] In their view, the secret of such an economic 'boom' was to be found in the growth of productivity of social labour thanks to the introduction of new techniques and in the increasing number of workers employed in material production.[44]

At the apex of the Cold War, economic performance became a fundamental ingredient in the political struggle between the two superpowers. Ideology also mattered. The difference between the USSR measures of material product and the GNP was due not only to different statistical components but also to profound conceptual distinctions. GNP had been invented to gauge the size and scope of market economies and was calculated in terms of market prices. Material product, on the contrary, reflected the characteristics of a command economy and inevitably privileged some economic activities (e.g. industrial production) at the expense of others (e.g. services), as the former were considered to constitute the backbone of the communist economy.[45] Moreover, in a non-market economy, political authorities set prices for most consumption commodities and this inevitably affected the final measurement.

For over four decades, these statistical differences triggered particular interest not only among economists and analysts, but also among the secret services of the US. Starting in 1950, the Central Intelligence Agency (CIA) began to investigate Soviet measures of national income with a view to discrediting their alleged growth rates and providing a more accurate assessment of the USSR's economic development and its projected potential expansion. As declared by Max Millikan, the first director of the CIA's Office of Research and Reports, foreign economic intelligence was essential to estimate the magnitude of present and future military threats (e.g. by assessing the resources available to other countries), to anticipate the intentions of potential enemies and undermine their capabilities and, most importantly, to project the relative strength of the West vis-à-vis the East.[46] As remarked by former CIA analyst James H. Noren, American policymakers were obsessed 'with the prospect that the USSR would overtake the US in terms of national output'[47] and this led to a specific policy framework to equip the secret services with all necessary resources to do the job as quickly and as effectively as possible. As Millikan put it, their job was to conduct a 'patient and thorough examination and analysis of the mass of detailed information available to us as to the present status and prospects of the Soviet economy', which 'may well be the most important research job there is in the country today'.[48] And, according to Princeton historian and CIA consultant Joseph Strayer, 'some of the most valuable intelligence papers ever written [are] those projecting the future economic growth of the USSR.'[49]

Among other things, CIA experts were interested in measuring the actual effectiveness with which a command economy allocated resources in order to estimate for how long the communist regime could guarantee acceptable living standards to the population. This was fundamental information to gauge the sustainability of the USSR economy and its resilience to popular unrest, both within the Soviet Union and among the countries of the Warsaw Pact. The CIA's work also focused on more technical issues, such as the actual weight of inflation and the contribution of foreign trade to Soviet national income (and how this was reflected in the changing of prices and availability of goods and services). Indeed, foreign trade accounting was particularly difficult for centrally planned economies because it was conducted in prices unrelated to those enforced domestically, which could have hidden effects on the final measures of national income.[50]

In what became a full-blown 'stats war', the CIA was tasked with producing data to discredit whatever new plan the Soviet leadership came up with. For example, when party leaders Nikita Khrushchev and then Leonid Brezhnev put forward their ambitious agricultural programmes in the 1950s and 1970s respectively, the CIA published reports to demonstrate how these production goals could not be met. When in 1958 the Central Committee of the Communist Party agreed on a five-year plan to boost investment, defence and internal consumption in an effort to maximize economic output, and when it declared that by 1970 the Soviet

Union would lead the world in both absolute and per capita output, providing its population with the highest living standards, the CIA promptly dissected the available information coming out of the USSR's records and pronounced these plans unfeasible.[51]

By showing gaps in the Soviet national accounts and by estimating a decline in GNP growth, the CIA reports did a great deal to ease concerns about the USSR's capacity to overtake the US as the largest economy in the world, a goal that Khrushchev had officially set for his country in a declaration to the Congress of the Communist Party in 1961. So, when the CIA reported that – according to their estimates – the actual increase in Soviet GNP for 1963 had been of only 2.5 per cent, US president Johnson dispatched a delegation to present the findings in West European capitals and reassure his allies.[52]

In 1982, the Joint Economic Committee of the US Congress published a volume prepared by the CIA entitled *Measures of Economic Growth and Development in the USSR (1950–1980)*, which contained the most detailed estimates of the growth of Soviet national income and its components ever published during a thirty-year period. These calculations estimated 'real' growth in the USSR at roughly half of the official rates and argued that, in the previous two decades, the Soviet economy had actually experienced a significant slowdown in economic growth. Such estimates were further confirmed at the end of the 1980s, when the CIA calculated that – for most of the post-war period – USSR per capita consumption had increased only by 2.9 per cent annually, compared with official estimates averaging around 4.5 per cent. At the same time, a number of studies disputed the accuracy of the CIA's estimates. According to research carried out by a former employee of the US Department of Commerce, 'the CIA may substantially underestimate the growth of the Soviet economy' in an effort to exaggerate 'difficulties facing the Soviet leadership in the economic sphere'. As the author of the study conceded, 'although these difficulties are real, and are reported extensively both in the Soviet press and in statistical sources, they might be less severe than as portrayed by CIA estimates.'[53]

Whether true or not, the CIA's allegations regarding the Soviet national accounts started reaping fruit. In the mid-1980s, the USSR government led by Mikhail Gorbachev introduced a comprehensive series of reforms to favour openness in public affairs, the so-called *glasnost*, which also resulted in major changes with regard to official statistics. Partly fuelled by the publication of the CIA's reports, a struggle broke out among the Soviet ruling elite. In an effort to discredit the country's previous leadership and pave the way for his programme of reforms, Gorbachev himself suggested that there had been little or no growth in the economy during the late Brezhnev years and criticized official statistics for hiding this.[54] Such a stance gave impetus to a number of revisionist studies on Soviet economic performance, some of which concluded that the economy had grown only a fraction of the officially reported rates. On the basis of admittedly rough calculations relying heavily on basic production series, new estimates indicated that the economy had grown only 500 to 600 per cent between 1928 and 1985, while the official records showed an 8,500 per cent increase.[55]

Building on the allegations put forward by the CIA, industrial production was also reported to be about one-fifth of the official records and, when compared with the US, the Soviet economy was found to be smaller and less efficient than suggested in official statistics.[56] Confirming the suspicion of US experts, a 1988 article documented the distortions in Goskomstat statistics, showing that the Soviet statistical office had largely ignored inflation in the prices of machinery, chemicals and consumer goods over the previous twenty years. Abel Aganbegyan, one of Gorbachev's main economic advisers, suggested that 'Soviet price statistics are inadequate and insufficiently account for hidden price increases through changes in the range of products, replacing cheaper with more expensive goods and without a corresponding improvement in their consumer quality.[57]

Because of mounting criticisms, the Soviet Union decided to abandon its previous methodology and began to compile official GNP statistics in 1988. The stated purpose was to supplement the Marxist–Leninist-based national income and gross social product with a new measure that would broaden and deepen the analysis of social reproduction, as well as facilitate international comparisons.[58] At the same time, it may not have been coincidental that the adoption of GNP held the promise of helping 'push up' the numbers of economic output because of the rapid growth of the service sector in the late 1980s. During this transition phase, Goskomstat reached out to American specialists, including the US Bureau of the Census and the Bureau of Economic Analysis, to help reform their statistical operations and improve data-gathering methods. Given its acquired expertise in this field, the CIA was instrumental in facilitating the transfer of knowledge and, in May 1989 its Office of Soviet Analysis held a seminar that focused on how to better prepare for the transition of the USSR to full GNP accounting.[59] After a few months, on 10 November, thousands of citizens gathered at the main checkpoints dividing East and West Berlin, in Germany. In a matter of hours, the 'wall' between capitalism and communism had fallen. Two years later, the Soviet Union collapsed and the new leadership cheerfully embraced the market economy.

Globalization of national income and the global economic crisis

With the incorporation of the USSR into the GNP world, the latter became the globally accepted measure of economic success. Through the United Nations, the SNA was exported to the rest of the world and methodological capacity was built in developing countries to collect regular statistics on economic performance. Over time, in response to policy needs and changes in the economy, the accounts have been expanded to provide, among other things, estimates of personal income, measures of real output and prices reflecting current expenditure patterns, quality-adjusted prices for high-tech goods and measures of banking output that recognize cash withdrawals, electronic funds transfers, as well as the wide range of services that most banks provide.

In 1991, the GNP was superseded by GDP, which is still the most popular acronym by which national income is commonly known. From 'national' the gross product became 'domestic'. Although this may look like an irrelevant shift that only insiders would care about, it indeed signalled an important political change. Traditional GNP referred to all goods and services produced by the residents of a given country, regardless of whether the 'income' was generated within or outside its borders. This meant that, for instance, the earnings of a multinational corporation were attributed to the country where the firm was owned and where the profits would eventually return. With the introduction of the gross 'domestic' product, this calculation changed completely. GDP is indeed territorially defined, which means that the income generated by foreign companies is 'formally' attributed to the country where it is generated, even though the profits may very well not remain there. This conceptual evolution (which of course altered existing statistics) was by and large responsible for the economic boom of many developing nations. Yet, it is obvious that the gains it revealed were more apparent than real. They may be reflected in the numbers and, perhaps, in the rhetoric of political leaders, but hardly in the daily experience of common citizens. Indeed, this statistical abstraction hides a basic fact: 'the nations of the North are walking off with the South's resources, and calling it a gain for the South.'[60]

In the mid-1990s, GDP established its authority as the over-arching parameter to guide economic policies in the European continent too. At the supranational level, this was done through the adoption of the Maastricht Treaty, which laid the groundwork for a gradual process of economic integration of the European 'region', and – most importantly – with the entry into force of the Stability and Growth Pact, which tied the government's capacity to sustain public welfare to the performance of GDP. Having embraced the neoliberal creed, Western European economies – traditionally inspired by a social democratic approach to po-litical economy – elevated GDP to the utmost criterion to judge not only economic success but also the affordability of social expenditure and investment. From then on, all European member states and their citizens came to accept that only if GDP went up could they afford to pay for schools, hospitals and social security. Should this not be case, European institutions would intervene to sanction governments that derailed from the GDP discipline: 'No GDP growth, no party'.

The pervasiveness of GDP also colonized the very lexicon of global governance. International clubs such as the G8, or the G20, were defined according to their members' contribution to global economic output. The definition of 'emerging markets' and 'emerging powers' was also dependent on a nation's current and projected GDP growth. For instance, the acronym 'BRIC' indicates the fast-growing economies of Brazil, Russia, India and China and was introduced in the international political debate by a 2001 report published by the investment bank Goldman Sachs.[61] Their analysis was based purely on GDP accounts and estimates of future projections, according to which the economic output of these four economies will be able to overtake the G8 by 2050 and thus create a new planetary leadership.

For the past three decades, GDP has been the key to success. Its underlying economic principles have contributed to splitting the planet into two worlds: the 'developed' and the 'developing' countries. Through the adoption of policies to sustain GDP, a country would not only reap alleged economic benefits but it would also see its geopolitical status increase. Similarly, sluggish GDP performance would throw a nation into a vicious circle of structural adjustments and macroeconomic reforms, mostly dictated by the World Bank and the International Monetary Fund, in partnership with international investors and financial markets. Paradoxically, the GDP mantra was imposed on poorer nations in spite of Kuznets' conclusions (as will be discussed in the following chapter) that the GDP approach should never be applied to countries largely dependent on informal economic structures.

In spite of the GDP boom and the creed of infinite economic growth, the 1990s were also characterized by profound social imbalances, a growing income gap and pervasive psychological distress, especially in the US. Looking at the recurrence of burnouts, divorces and the rise of alcoholism (and drug abuse), the Clinton administration repeatedly affirmed that Americans may be simply suffering the anxieties of adjustment to a wondrous new economy. Speaking in similar terms, Alan Greenspan, the then chairman of the Federal Reserve Board, told an official gathering in San Francisco in 1994 that it should be expected that the economy's dynamism would create 'frictions and human stress.' When confronted with opinion polls showing that millions of Americans were worried about increasing inequality, he added: 'There seemingly inexplicably remains an extraordinarily deep-rooted foreboding about the future.... But the optimism that has characterized Americans through the generations will again become predominant.'[62] According to a study by political scientists Paul Pierson and Jacob Hacker, not only did the pro-growth policies of the 1980s and 1990s produce a widening gap between the richest and the poorest in America, but the trend was further exacerbated after the turn of the millennium thanks to the growing capacity of US business to influence politics and governmental strategies.[63]

In spite of alarming signals coming from many directions, in 1999 the US government declared GDP 'one of the greatest inventions of the 20th century'.[64] The US Department of Commerce, which, ever since Kuznets developed the first calculations, had been producing the GDP official statistics under the guidance of Milton Gilbert, named the development of the national income and product accounts 'its achievement of the century'. On that occasion, the former US secretary of commerce William M. Daley declared that 'since the end of World War II, when the GDP accounts were more fully developed and in wider use, the boom and bust swings are much less severe. ... They have had a very positive effect on America's economic well-being, by providing a steady stream of very useful economic data.'[65] In the words of Nobel prizewinner James Tobin, GDP is the 'right concept of economy-wide output, accurately measured. The U.S. and the world rely on it to tell where we are in the business cycle and to estimate long-run growth.'[66]

According to US senator Paul Sarbanes, 'The GDP accounts provide Congress and the rest of government with vital signs on our economy's health. We are making better economic policy today because the GDP accounts give us a better understanding of what policies work.'[67] Yet, only three years later, in 2002, after a number of major corporate scandals (such as those involving the energy giant Enron and the telecommunications company WorldCom), Senator Sarbanes sponsored the Sarbanes–Oxley Act setting stricter rules for the business sector. For President George W. Bush, who signed it into law, the Sarbanes–Oxley Act introduced 'the most far-reaching reforms of American business practices since the time of Franklin D. Roosevelt. ... The era of low standards and false profits is over.'[68]

But was it? In 2007–08, the world entered a new devastating financial crisis that soon triggered a seemingly endless global economic downturn. The US housing market, which had been one of the major drivers of the country's economic growth, collapsed in a few months and plunged the stock exchange into disarray. What was soon to become the largest recession since the Great Depression of the 1930s also had a knock-on effect on Europe and many developing countries, causing multiple recessions and the constant fear of a prolonged global stagnation. The long-term consequences of this Great Recession are hard to predict, but governmental responses pointed to a general downsizing of the public sector that inevitably resulted in massive lay-offs and cuts in the social sector and welfare systems. The European continent, historically shielded by stronger social safety nets and stricter public control systems over the economy, plummeted into a profound sovereign debt crisis. Ever since, entire countries have been on the verge of economic collapse and the social unrest is unprecedented.

While GDP served the interests of political and economic elites for several decades, it appears to have run out of steam, at least in the so-called Western world. Since 2007, estimates and measurements of GDP have been released and revised several times, as governments have tried to manipulate data and results for political purposes. In 2008, the *Wall Street Journal* reported on the US Department of Commerce's admission that estimates and calculations of GDP expansion had been wrong for the previous four years and had to be revised downward, thus pointing to a probable recession already in 2007 despite most politicians' rather optimistic representations of the state of the American economy.[69] The Department also admitted that most of its estimates 'are based on source data that are incomplete or subject to further revision' and that recessions pose 'significant challenges to the accuracy of economic indicators', including those that are used as source data for the early GDP estimates: 'During recessions, some firms go out of business, some may only partially complete surveys, and some may choose to not respond at all to voluntary surveys.[70] Reflecting on the data inconsistencies and other types of errors increasingly affecting the calculation of GDP, researchers at the Federal Reserve recently suggested a minor – but politically relevant – revision: to replace it with its income-based alter ego, namely gross domestic income (GDI).[71] Politically, this idea appeared rather palatable to the US administration, given that GDI painted a more positive picture of the long-awaited economic recovery. In the first quarter of 2011, the real GDP growth estimates showed an annualized growth of 0.4 per cent, while the GDI showed 2.4 per cent. In 2012, the Bureau of Economic Analysis reported that, in the fourth quarter of 2011, GDI had increased by 4.4 per cent vis-à-vis a 3 per cent growth in GDP.[72]

In February 2008, then French president Nicolas Sarkozy established a Commission on the Measurement of Economic Progress and Performance, chaired by renowned economists Joseph Stiglitz, Amartya Sen and Jean-Paul Fitoussi. Sarkozy was apparently unsatisfied with the state of statistical information about the economy and expected the commission to identify the limits of GDP as an indicator of economic performance and social progress, including the problems with its measurement.[73] Between 2008 and 2009, the GDP of France had contracted by over four points and the country only came out of a recession in 2010, just before the European crisis sank the continent's economic outlook once again.[74]

The OECD and the European Union promoted a new initiative by the name of 'Beyond GDP', and in 2009 the European Commission released a formal 'communication' entitled *GDP and Beyond: Measuring Progress in a Changing World*.[75] In late 2010, amid retrenchments, skyrocketing tuition fees for students and the reform of the National Health Service, British prime minister David Cameron called on the UK Office for National Statistics to complement the ever-more gloomy calculations of quarterly GDP trends with more general references to the 'happiness' of his fellow citizens. Speaking at the Google Zeitgeist Europe conference, he added: 'Wellbeing can't be measured by money or traded in markets. It's about the beauty of our surroundings, the quality of our culture and, above all, the strength of our relationships. Improving our society's sense of wellbeing is, I believe, the central political challenge of our times.'[76] A couple of months later, the US government followed suit. Funded by the Department of Health and Human Services, a panel of experts in psychology and economics, including Nobel laureate Daniel Kahneman, began to define reliable measures of 'subjective well-being' to be incorporated into official statistics.[77] President Obama officially welcomed the effort, which was also sponsored by his chief economic adviser, the Princeton economist Alan Krueger, who co-authored a 2009 paper proposing 'a new approach for measuring features of society's subjective well-being'.[78] Finally, in April 2012, the UN secretary general Ban Ki-Moon participated in a conference titled 'Happiness and Well-being: Defining a New Economic Paradigm', hosted by the representation of Bhutan at the UN headquarters in New York. In his opening remarks, he said:

> Gross Domestic Product (GDP) has long been the yardstick by which economies and politicians have been measured. Yet it fails to take into account the social and environmental costs of so-called progress.... We need a new economic paradigm that recognizes the parity between the three pillars of sustainable development. Social, economic and environmental well-being are indivisible. Together they define gross global happiness.[79]

The greatest invention of the twentieth century?

GDP had a profound impact on our societies for most of the twentieth century and still drives economic policies today. From the 1950s to the 1990s, the measurement of national income was refined several times in accordance with changing political and economic interests. For instance, in the late 1950s to early 1960s, the widespread pressure to stimulate economic growth (and identify the best sources of growth) led to the development of official 'input–output' tables, capital stock estimates, and more detailed local personal income estimates. In the 1970s, accelerating inflation prompted the introduction of new measures of prices and inflation-adjusted output. In the 1980s, the internationalization of trade in services led to an expansion of this component into the calculation of national income.

One of the more subtle consequences of this process has been the increasing importance that economists have acquired in designing national policies throughout the world. Before the Second World War, economists were rarely quoted in the media, but ever since the invention of GDP and its quarterly updates, economic experts of all sorts have become essential players in public debate and, more often than not, they have been viewed as the holders of some type of canonical truth. As remarked by Paul A. Volcker, former chairman of the Federal Reserve, 'For decades, the Department of Commerce, in maintaining the statistics, has also nurtured and protected a group of economists that have made an enormous contribution to independent, authoritative, and timely analysis. It is of great benefit to the United States and unmatched in the world.'[80]

Undoubtedly, the biggest change brought about by GDP regarded society as a whole. Economic categories such as workers, entrepreneurs, professionals, farmers or social categories such as parents and children, as well as political categories such as citizens, were all conflated into two 'camps': producers and consumers. Given that the GDP approach saw consumption as the driver of prosperity, society itself was shaped accordingly and economic policies were designed to push for all types of consumerism. While military conflict had marked the success of GDP as a political instrument, the post-war system of mass consumption sealed its grip on society as a tool of economic hegemony: 'Our young men had marched off to war; now Americans were marching off to the malls that eventually covered the land.'[81] And this intimate relationship between war and consumption did not fade away in times of peace. Between 1948 and 1989, American economic growth was largely dependent upon military spending. As demonstrated by economic historian Robert Higgs, most positive and negative years in US economic performance are 'merely because of variations in defense spending – a type of spending with a very tenuous relation to the well-being of consumers, investors, and the beneficiaries of governmentally purchased civilian goods and services'.[82]

The global financial crisis that began in 2007–08 appears to have opened up new opportunities to erode the supreme power of GDP. Different political, economic and social camps have criticized this indicator because of what it measures and because of what it does not measure. Most importantly, civil society groups and individual citizens have been challenging not just the 'number' but also the political and economic interests it has been serving ever since its creation. It is from this popular struggle that a new model of society may begin.

CHAPTER 2

The Frankenstein syndrome

For this I had deprived myself of rest and health. I had
desired it with an ardour that far exceeded moderation; but
now that I had finished, the beauty of the dream vanished,
and breathless horror and disgust filled my heart.... I lived
in daily fear, lest the monster whom I had created should
perpetrate some new wickedness.

Mary Shelley, *Frankenstein*

The invention of GDP marked a fundamental turning point in
the evolution of economic thinking and its relationship with
policymaking. As some have suggested, the very idea of economic
growth was 'in an important sense a discovery of economics
after the Second World War'.[1] Indeed, mainstream economic
analysis such as classical and neoclassical theory had been
hitherto uncomfortable with phenomena of continuous change.[2]
Also Keynesian theory fell in the same tradition, attempting to
apply the static equilibrium theory to the essentially dynamic
problem of saving and capital accumulation. As discussed in the
previous chapter, Kuznets' work on US national income, coupled
with similar efforts conducted by Meade and Stone in the UK,
opened up a new horizon not only for economic theory but also

for its applied analysis, providing a wealth of data to test traditional approaches and refute or confirm deep-seated convictions. Thanks to their contribution, neoclassical growth theory became the new mainstream approach to economics and successfully made its way into textbooks the world over. As a consequence, 'evangelistic worshippers'[3] of GDP growth took over not only academic research, but also public debate. For instance, Arthur Okun, the chairman of the Council of Economic Advisers under US president Johnson, elevated GDP to the key parameter to drive macroeconomic policy and fight unemployment. He coined the so-called Okun's Law (which should be rather considered a 'rule of thumb', given that it is based only on some partial empirical observations rather than a consistent theory), which maintained that a 3 per cent increase in GDP generates a 1 per cent increase in employment. Interestingly, this allegedly intimate connection between GDP and job creation (a fundamental 'preoccupation' of politicians) made it largely undisputed into mainstream policymaking and affected the thinking of, among others, powerful professional economists such as the current chairman of the Federal Reserve, Ben Bernanke.[4] From the 1960s on, GDP conquered the political scene and affirmed itself as the supreme indicator of modernity and progress. Everything else (e.g. environmental sustainability, social justice, poverty eradication) was sacrificed on the altar of economic growth. As argued by the magazine *Foreign Policy* in a 2011 article, GDP became 'the ultimate measure of a country's overall welfare, a window into an economy's soul, the statistic to end all statistics... the defining indicator of the last century'.[5]

Yet, according to Nobel prizewinning economists William Nordhaus and James Tobin the conventional approach endorsed by most economists and politicians depicted GDP growth as 'a routine process of replication', a linear process of societal improvement, as opposed to the convulsive structural, technological and social changes described by traditional political economists such as Adam Smith, Karl Marx and Joseph Schumpeter. For Nordhaus and Tobin, the neoclassical growth theory 'conceals, either in aggregation or in the abstract generality of multisector models, all the drama of the events – the rise and fall of products, technologies, industries, and the accompanying transformations of the spatial and occupational distribution of the population'.[6] Indeed, between 1960 and 1990, American GDP nearly tripled and total social spending by all levels of government (measured in constant 1990 dollars) rose from $143.73 billion to $787 billion (a more than fivefold increase). Yet, during the same thirty-year period there was a 560 per cent increase in violent crime, a 419 per cent increase in illegitimate births, a quadrupling in divorce rates, a tripling of the percentage of children living in single-parent homes and more than a 200 per cent increase in the teenage suicide rate.[7] In the late 1980s, just before his death and after two tenures of GDP worshipper President Reagan, the novelist Walker Percy was asked what concerned him most about America's future. He answered: 'Probably the fear of seeing America with all its great strength and beauty and freedom ... gradually subside into decay through default and be defeated, not by the Communist movement ... but from within by weariness, boredom, cynicism, greed and, in the end, helplessness.'[8] There were some scholars, though, who tried their best to warn society about the dangerous consequence of a blind devotion to GDP growth. Among them was Kuznets himself.

Taming the monster

Until the 1950s, Simon Kuznets had been an indefatigable supporter of national income statistics. As a scholar and adviser to policymakers, he had coordinated research projects to further improve the measurement of national wealth that ultimately led to the development of income tables for the US that extended back to 1869. He had also assembled estimates in constant prices for tens of other countries dating back to 1841.[9] Moreover, he had successfully employed national product figures to compare levels of output and income in virtually all the nations of the world, from the economically most advanced to the least industrialized. After this initial period of euphoria, though, Kuznets started to look at his 'creation' with increasing suspicion. Among others, he began to focus on problems of income distribution with a view to highlighting the complications affecting redistribution of resources during any growth process.[10] He was concerned about the fact that, because of the way in which the national accounts had been designed, an accretion of luxury expenses at the top of the income scale of a nation would offset a drop of purchasing power at the bottom. Indeed, a country in which the richest become richer and the poorest become poorer can perform very well in terms of overall GDP growth. But this imbalance is obviously problematic in terms of real economic performance. In such cases, GDP looks more like a 'statistical laundry' that conceals the increase in inequality, a process that has become quite common in most advanced economies. For instance, in a 2008 report titled *Growing Unequal*, the OECD attested that income inequality in the most developed countries had become higher than it had been in the mid-1980s, a trend further corroborated by 2011 data, in spite of sustained growth and rather exceptional GDP performances.[11]

Kuznets also raised doubts about the reliability of national income measures, for which data was often missing, and took great pains to single out the disparate sources of error in international comparisons. Importantly, he noted that growth of GDP in industrial countries might be easily overestimated by counting in goods and services whose sole purpose is to offset the drawbacks of industrialization, such as the increasing cost of traffic, pollution and security. At the same time, the level of output in developing countries may be underestimated owing to variations in the extent to which the market operates in less industrialized nations and the more widespread availability of free resources. Moreover, he raised concerns about using rates of foreign exchange as indicators of relative purchasing power and warned that the comparison of prices may pose intricate problems.[12] All these issues would constitute, as we will discuss later on, the backbone of the more fundamental critique of GDP as both a reliable measure of economic performance and an indicator of general welfare.

In 1962, at the height of the GDP hype, Kuznets realized the many ways in which his indicator was being misread and manipulated for political purposes. He acknowledged that 'the welfare of a national can scarcely be inferred from a measure of national income' and emphasized the fact that policymakers should distinguish between the mere 'quantity' of economic growth and its actual 'quality' in order to clarify what type of growth they want to achieve and 'for what'.[13]

To his credit, Kuznets had already raised some critical points regarding measurements of national income as early as 1937. For starters, he had provided an important distinction between net and gross product. The net product, he had clarified, is a more accurate measure because 'the value of output of all commodities and services is reduced by the value of commodities (fuel, raw materials and capital equipment) consumed in the process of production'.[14] By contrast, the gross product 'is not fully adjusted for the value of commodities consumed'.[15] As a consequence, while net product is unequivocal, there may be different types of gross product depending on what duplications are included in the final calculation. Is the value of the coal consumed in the production process of a machine counted extra or included in the value of the machine? Is the value of the machine used to produce an automobile counted separately or subsumed under the price of the vehicle? Each level of duplication generates a different 'gross' value and each specific industry (or sector) may be interested in adopting one type of system rather than another to showcase its relative weight in the national economic output.[16] In spite of this important distinction, gross measures have ended up prevailing over net measures due to the 'difficulties and lags in estimating capital consumption', which have resulted in GDP (which could be calculated quarterly) becoming 'the popular statistic' notwithstanding its inherent limitations as an accurate measure of economic production.[17]

Moreover, if the depreciation of machinery and capital is subtracted from GDP, should not the same also apply to the wearing out of people? Indeed, the system of production takes its toll not only on 'things' but also on 'human beings'. This is what Kuznets called the 'reverse side of income'; that is, 'the intensity and unpleasantness of effort going into the earning of income'.[18] However, national income focuses only on satisfying consumers' demands for commodities and services: 'the burden of work and discomfort are ignored'.[19] At the same time, the national product does not represent all the means of purchase that are available to individuals during any given year. The power of individuals to buy in markets depends not only upon the current flow of income but also on the possibility of exploiting other sources, such as assets and credit facilities: 'This suggests that measures of the national product, in order to be adequate as a gauge of the performance of the economic system even in terms of the market place, must be supplemented by a study of wealth and capital structure.'[20]

Since the early formulations of national income, Kuznets made it plain that his gross national product was just a measurement of market transactions rather than a comprehensive assessment of the overall production of an economic system. 'If market is understood broadly as the meeting place of all buyers and sellers', he wrote in the late 1930s, then gross product 'excludes the results of other activities that may supply utilities but are outside the market mechanism.'[21] Thus, his estimates of national income included 'payments as wages, salaries, dividends and interest' but did not consider returns to individuals from their activity within the family system 'or from other pursuits that are not, strictly speaking, working for the market'.[22] His indicator did not measure *all* the goods and services produced in the nation, since – because of its own statistical design – it did not account for 'a large volume of services and a substantial volume of commodities produced outside the economic system proper' and neglected '[t]he great contribution to our stock of utilities made within the family system and by numerous activities of mankind engaged in the ordinary processes of life'.[23] Among others, this deficiency generated the evident paradox that the same household service would be counted as adding to GDP when provided by a waged domestic but not when rendered by a housewife. Moreover, Kuznets remarked that the distinction between proper market activities and 'other utility producing activities' is influenced by culture, institutional conditions and political views, and therefore it shifts 'from time to time and from country to country', thus limiting the application of this methodology in international comparisons and over time. Attempts at retroactively measuring national income in the 1800s, for instance, bumped against the fact that GDP estimates turned out to be lower not only because the economies of the time were smaller than those of the 1900s, but also because – due to the specific conditions of those societies – most non-market-based economic functions, such as subsistence farming, were still widespread. Similarly, many societies in the contemporary world intentionally keep a number of productive functions, from community work to foster care and education, separate from the market arena. But since GDP is a measure of how 'marketized' a given society is, then it goes without saying that national income estimates fare rather poorly as 'approximations to the value of the total stock of commodities and services produced' in nations where economies are intentionally or structurally under-marketized.[24]

Although he opted for a strict market-based approach, Kuznets' definition of national income invariably incorporated some basic moral requirements. In his first collection of national accounts, he remarked that national income cannot include 'activities that have been explicitly recognized by society at large, overtly in the form of legal prohibition, not only as unproductive but also as distinctly harmful' as well as 'activities that while legal, represent largely shifts of income among individuals rather than additions to the command over goods'.[25] These convictions led him to exclude profits stemming from crimes such as theft, robbery, prostitution and drug trafficking. To assume that such expenditures added to national income would indeed undercut the rationale for making them illegal in the first place. At the same time, though, Kuznets was aware of the sometimes arbitrary demarcation between legality and illegality. In particular he was worried that such criteria would give governments a significant discretion in filtering what gets counted as national income and what does not. Kuznets had lived through the transition from Prohibition to the legalization of alcohol and knew all too well how national income statistics could be surreptitiously affected by shifts in legislation without any real change in the economy. For instance, the income of official casinos was included in the gross national product, while illegal gambling was taken out. But from an economic point of view, what did legal gambling add to national income that its illegal version did not? Or what was the social and economic impact of legal prostitution as opposed to the illegal one? Kuznets was also conscious of the fact that not 'all lawful pursuits are necessarily serviceable from the social viewpoint'.[26] In particular, he was hostile to the idea of including the speculative gains obtained through financial transactions in the computation of national income. After the financial turmoil of the Great Depression, he had come to believe that financial speculation is derived 'from the sale of assets that can in no way be interpreted as resulting from skill in the performance of any useful functions that speculative markets may be presumed to render'.[27]

All these exclusions from the final calculation of national income were not taken lightly, as they also restrained and burdened the methodology. Indeed, one of the appeals of the GDP design was its circular distribution. The formula designed by Kuznets guaranteed that national product could be measured at the level of production, income or consumption and, at least in theory, it should always bring the same results.[28] But, of course, the more economic activities one excludes from the definition, the more discrepancies will emerge across the different types of calculations: if the production of certain commodities and services is excluded from the first measurement (production), then it is impossible to 'include in individuals' incomes the compensation received from these activities, nor, when we use the third definition, can we include in the value of products consumed the expenditures on these activities'.[29] If the income generated by an illegal prostitute, by an underground gambling house or by a financial speculator is excluded from the national income produced, then one must find a way to take out this money also when it is spent in legal purchases or to pay legitimate salaries. Because, at the end of the day, street prostitutes still use their money to buy bread and milk. Although this was no easy task for Kuznets and his team, he was nevertheless convinced that 'to include them in the national product totals would make it impossible to interpret the latter as the contribution of the economic system that appears useful to society at large'.[30]

Kuznets' view of national product was of course rather different from the idea of GDP that eventually prevailed. In 1946, he wrote that the specific design of gross product, which ignores a large and important part of a society's economic and social life, 'warns us against too easy an acceptance of the thesis that a high national income is the sole desideratum in theory or the dominant motive in fact in a nation's economy'.[31] Although he was a man of crude statistics, he could not accept that national income guided economic policy without being complemented or strengthened by additional measures of welfare.

This ambivalence was picked up on by Stanford economist Moses Abramovitz in 1959, in what was to become the first systematic critique of GDP and the national accounts.[32] He argued that studies of economic growth 'almost invariably treat long-term change in national product as the most basic index of national economic achievement',[33] although national product is by no means an accurate or comprehensive measure of economic welfare. Besides reiterating most of Kuznets' warnings regarding the use of GDP as a tool for designing economic policy, Abramovitz identified a set of additional deficiencies, including the distinction between goods and nongoods, the separation of intermediate goods (those used in the production process) from final goods (those purchased for consumption), and the use of market prices as the valuation criteria. For him, all these methodological choices appeared to neglect the important recognition that

> [i]n the course of industrialization, certain goods that once were free have become scarce, or vice versa, because the sphere of household and other unpaid production has shrunk in favor of commercial production, because output includes capital formation as well as goods consumed immediately by individuals, and because of the great rise in government output for which the test of consumer demand in the market place is not available.[34]

With his pivotal reflection on the blurred distinction between intermediate and final goods, Abramovitz anticipated an important criticism to national income that would then be reiterated, among other things, by Nordhaus and Tobin in the early 1970s. For instance, some consumer outlays (e.g. the costs of commuting to work) or most government 'purchases' (e.g. police services) are only instrumental in that they do not add to the utility of individuals: they can be considered rather as 'the necessary over-head costs of a complex industrial nation-state'.[35] Conceptually, therefore, these outlays should be excluded from a measure that aims to account for the overall economic progress of a country. Yet, not only have these 'regrettable expenses' been also included in national income, but – according to Nordhaus and Tobin – they accounted for over 16 per cent of gross domestic product during America's economic boom, from the early 1930s to the mid-1960s.[36] Almost two decades later, the German economist Christian Leipert argued that national income should exclude all transportation costs, repair works, environmental protection expenses, security services, prisons, and most health as well as legal costs from its final total. In his estimates for West Germany in 1989, he found that these 'unfortunate' expenses exceeded 10 per cent of GDP, which he considered likely to be 'only the tip of the iceberg'.[37]

Building on an argument initially put forward by Kuznets,[38] Abramovitz also highlighted how inadequate (and potentially dangerous) was the decision to measure the value of goods and services in terms of market prices. In theory, market prices should by and large correspond to the marginal utility that goods and services bring to individual consumers: that is, the price is the best estimate of these items' exchange value. Yet, in most real economies, there are many prices that are not at all (or only partly) affected by the preferences and priorities of consumers, es-pecially in the field of capital investment and government outlays, which over the years have become fundamental components of GDP. Particularly in the case of capital investment, Abramovitz put forward an argument that appears extremely prescient of the current status of financial markets in the twenty-first century, with all its derivatives and other complex forms of investment schemes. According to his reasoning, in 'the course of the last 150 years, it is clear that a growing proportion of private investment has come to be made by managers of firms who are not the beneficial owners of the capital'.[39] The development of the capital market has meant that the rates at which corporate managers discount future possibilities for futurity and risk (and thus prices) are not equal to the rates that beneficial owners would apply. The function of the capital market, from one point of view, is to shift the investment of funds into the hands of 'experts' who discount the future 'more optimistically and a lower rate of time preference than do the savers themselves'.[40] Consequently, the output of the future is made greater, but riskier, than savers would think worthwhile.

Even though at the time of his writing financial markets had not yet known the complex evolutions of our recent years, Abramovitz could already sense that GDP was grossly inadequate to measure the real value of capital investment considering 'the elaborate and indirect processes of security trading and speculation by which savings are channeled to investors and securities to intermediate credit institutions and thence, in changed forms, to savers'.[41] In his view, the difficulty with the valuation of government output presented similar problems. Ideally, the goods and services provided by government should add to the national income at prices proportionate to their marginal utility to consumers. However, GDP assesses the value of this category at the cost to the government, which – by definition – is not set by market processes. There are technical and moral reasons why this is the case. First of all, most things provided by government 'have been brought into the government because the market process would itself be inefficient'.[42] Services such as road maintenance, national security, education, health care and the like are intentionally

kept within the government's remit because of specific social and
political priorities, which consider markets to be not sufficiently
efficient and trustworthy to do the job. Although this ensures
public ownership over certain areas of the economy, it cannot be
said that the prices paid for such goods and services are necessarily determined within a competitive market framework. As a
consequence, the impact of these prices on GDP is suspect. For
many of these items, the government and the supplier compose a
bilateral monopoly, and the prices reflect exclusively the relative
bargaining power of the transactors rather than the marginal
utility or the preferences of the final consumers.[43] Thus, there
is no guarantee that the price paid by government reflects the
optimal price that citizens (or, rather, consumers in the GDP
lingo) would have paid for the same goods or services. Moreover,
prices (both in government and in the market) can be easily affected by taxation, subsidies, lobbying, cartels, monopolies, not
to speak of political allegiances that can afford certain industries
preferential treatments not available to competitors.

The volatility of prices as criteria to establish the contribution of a given good or service to the national income is also
affected by labour productivity and technological advancements.
Nowadays, a brand new automobile costs proportionally much
less than it cost twenty or thirty years ago, mainly due to increased efficiency in both labour and technology. By contrast, it
still takes four violinists about ten minutes to perform Beethoven's
String Quartet No. 4 in C minor, just as it did when the German
composer was still alive. This phenomenon is known in economics as the Baumol's cost disease, which postulates that, in certain
sectors of the economy, costs and prices tend to grow regardless
of productivity, while in others they tend to experience significant
reductions.[44] The information and communication technology
is, perhaps, the sector in which variations in prices have been
the most evident in the past decades. In 1996, for instance, a

commission of experts constituted by the US Senate reported that the conventional parameter to measure inflation, the so-called consumer price index, regularly overestimated inflation partly because of biases in the price indexes for ICT products, such as personal computers and cellular phones.[45] By contrast, the debate in Europe has tended to go the opposite way: official price statistics have been criticized for underestimating inflation, partly due to the tendency of official statisticians to over-adjust for quality improvements, thereby painting too rosy a picture of citizens' real income.[46]

High-tech products are indeed characterized by fast rotation of goods, significant leaps in quality (not automatically reflected in the price) and short product life cycles. If GDP has to avoid the evident bias of downplaying the economic weight of these items just because their improvement in quality is not linearly reflected in the price, then statistics have to be manipulated. To this end, statisticians have adopted GDP 'deflators' that are generally based on so-called hedonic regressions, which allow for the recalculation of prices taking into consideration the actual quality improvements (rather than the nominal market value). In the early 1990s, the US Bureau of Labour Statistics began publishing quality-adjusted producer price indexes for computers and peripheral equipment, while in 1997 the Bureau of Economic analysis introduced a hedonic price index for digital telephone systems.[47] Ever since, hedonic prices have mushroomed in a variety of sectors (from residential housing to photocopy machines, faxes and all types of software) and currently account for about 20 per cent of nominal GDP, which is a very significant amount by all standards. A critical problem is that each statistical agency has adopted different methods for calculating the relevant deflator, thus generating discrepancies and inconsistencies across countries and over time.[48] Furthermore, some of these techniques rely on subjective assessments, generally provided by producers and users, to gauge the dollar estimate of the change in quality embedded in the new product, which gives some industries an undue influence on the final calculation of real GDP. As Abramovitz rightly pointed out long before these issues were formally raised in official circles, the use of prices as value weights in the measurement of national income poses insurmountable problems, 'practically' and 'conceptually', which should not only reduce the influence of GDP estimates in the design of public policies, but also lead to a fundamental re-examination of mainstream economic analysis.[49]

According to the website Shadow Government Statistics, various inflation distortions and methodological changes have resulted in a systematic upside bias in the official GDP reports of the US government. Figure 2.1 compares the official figures produced by the Bureau of Economic Analysis with those adjusted for what the analysts believe to be the government's statistical 'manipulations'. The discrepancy between the two curves shows that official and adjusted GDP estimates have grown significantly different since the mid-1980s. Quite interestingly, according to this analysis, the real recession would have already started in the early 2001 and not only in 2008, as reported by government.

Abramovitz's final criticism regards the usage of GDP as an indicator of economic well-being. In light of the growth of large cities and the radical improvements in transportation and communication, Abramovitz argued that understanding private consumption as the maximization of individual utility may mislead in the assessment of welfare, given that the consumption patterns of one individual are increasingly likely to affect the welfare of another. Economists normally suppose that individual satisfactions are independent of the levels of income and consumption enjoyed by others. By contrast, our wants for goods are, to some degree, '*competitive*, and few would deny that a considerable part of our drive for income is derived from a desire for distinction'.[50]

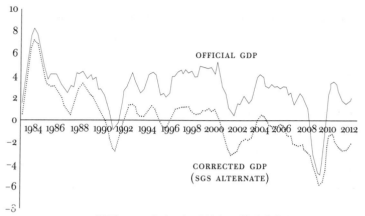

FIGURE 2.1   GDP growth in the USA: official GDP versus
distortion-adjusted estimates (% change)

Note: Official GDP estimates come from the Bureau of Economic analysis. The Shadow
Government Statistics Alternate GDP reflects the inflation-adjusted, or real, year-
to-year GDP change, adjusted for distortions in US government inflation usage and
methodological changes that have resulted in a built-in upside bias to official reporting.
The GDP headline number refers to the most recent quarter's annualized quarter-to-
quarter rate of change (what that quarter's % quarter-to-quarter change would translate
into if compounded for four consecutive quarters). This can mean that the latest quarter
can be reported with a positive annualized growth rate, while the actual annual rate of
change is negative. Such was the case for the third quarter of 2009. For more information
on the methodology see www.shadowstats.com.

It follows that, even if one accepts that extra income may provide
additional satisfaction to the individual, it will never be able to
do the same for the community at large, given that the satisfactions of some will be the cause of the dissatisfactions of others.
The interconnectedness among people should, therefore, force
economists to rethink the criteria of private marginal utility and
take into more serious consideration concepts such as 'social
marginal utility'. Moreover, there is 'empirical evidence' showing
that the utility added by national income 'diminishes as the level
of income increases'.[51] According to Abramovitz, the significance
of additional income for welfare becomes progressively weaker
'as industrialization proceeds', 'as per capita income rises', 'as

the options in consumption become greater', and 'as goods come more and more to have symbolic rather than material significance'.[52] Consequently,

> consumption may be self-defeating after a point, for this idea implies that the urgency of additional goods for satisfying solid needs becomes smaller and smaller, until at last the sole significance of increments is to avoid disappointing the established expectations they themselves create.[53]

Abramovitz's conclusion therefore is that any attempt to use national product estimates as indexes of economic welfare 'clearly runs into serious problems', some of which are simply difficult, while 'others seem beyond solution'.[54] GDP is fundamentally ahistorical in so far as it forces us to believe that human progress has not experienced important alterations in the composition of production, in the role of household and commercial economies, and in the rise of government as an economic agent. Moreover, it wants us to regard market prices as the most accurate representation of the inherent value of goods and services, in spite of the fact that prices are imperfect weights and, above all, are constantly manipulated by market and political interests.

Most political leaders have generally praised GDP as the solution to society's deepest problems over the course of the twentieth century, despite its profound limitations as an indicator of economic performance, let alone its inadequacies in measuring well-being. According to British economist Andrew J. Oswald,

> Every day, in every industrialised country of the world, journalists and politicians give out a conscious and unconscious message. It is that better economic performance means more happiness for a nation. This idea is rarely questioned. We feel we would be more cheery if our boss raised our pay, and assume that countries must be roughly the same.[55]

Yet, since the mid-1900s, numerous studies have demonstrated that there is no significant correlation between GDP growth and

happiness, at least in so far as individuals perceive it. Building
on Abramovitz's analysis, the economist Richard A. Easterlin of
the University of Southern California demonstrated that, after a
moderate level of income is reached, perceived happiness does
not increase with GDP. In a pivotal paper published in 1974,
Easterlin conducted the first empirical assessment of national
income on individual happiness and concluded that 'economic
growth does not raise a society to some ultimate state of plenty.
Rather, the growth process itself engenders ever-growing wants
that lead it ever onward.'[56] Twenty years later, in an updated
study, he reached similar conclusions:

> Will raising the incomes of all increase the happiness of all? The
> answer to this question can now be given with somewhat greater
> assurance than twenty years ago. ... It is 'no'. ... Put generally,
> happiness, or subjective well-being, varies directly with one's
> own income and inversely with the incomes of others. Raising
> the incomes of all does not increase the happiness of all, because
> the positive effect of higher income on subjective well-being is
> offset by the negative effect of higher living level norms brought
> about by the growth in incomes generally.[57]

What became known as the Easterlin Paradox seemed confirmed by public opinion surveys across a number of countries
worldwide. Although American GDP per capita more than doubled
from the Second World War until the early 1990s, there was no
empirical evidence of any improvement in perceived happiness.[58]
In Western Europe, personal satisfaction drifted upward in some
countries and downward in others, with little or no trend.[59]
Between the 1950s and the early 1990s, real per capita income in
Japan multiplied fivefold, propelling Japan to a living level equal
to about two-thirds that of the US.[60] Consumer durables such as
washing machines, refrigerators and television sets, found in few
homes at the start of the period, became well nigh universal, and
car ownership soared from 1 to about 60 per cent of households.[61]

Despite this unprecedented three-decade advance in GDP, there was no reported improvement in subjective well-being.[62]

In 1997, the Easterlin Paradox was tested with more recent and comprehensive data, but the results were only slightly more optimistic. Reported happiness in the US had gone up fractionally since the post-war period, while levels of 'satisfaction with life' in Europe were only slightly higher than twenty years earlier, although a number of countries showed significant falls. At the same time, the number of men committing suicide had increased in Western nations since the 1970s and richer countries showed overall higher suicide rates than poorer countries. The conclusion was that, possibly, 'economic progress buys only a small amount of extra happiness'.[63]

GDP versus society and the environment

National income accounts largely ignore the many sources of utility or disutility that are not associated with market transactions or measured by the market value of goods and services. According to Nordhaus and Tobin, the omission of leisure and nonmarket productive activity from measures of production conveys the impression that economists are 'blindly materialistic'. Yet, common sense tells us that welfare is likely to rise, even while GDP falls, 'as the result of voluntary choices to work for pay fewer hours per week, weeks per year, years per lifetime'.[64] In the 1970s, for instance, some 40 per cent of the population in the US constituted the labour force. On average, these people devoted 35 to 40 per cent of their waking time to work. Hence, employment – as directly reflected in the national product statistics – accounted for only 15 per cent of the population's total waking time. The other 85 per cent of total waking time was accounted for by leisure and by all the waking time of persons not formally employed, such as students, children, retirees, housewives, and so on.[65] Ever since, leisure activities and free time have become more and more important to individuals, especially in industrialized nations. Yet, most of these activities, unless they involve some type of monetary earning or spending, are largely neglected by GDP. As remarked by Nordhaus and Tobin, 'If one of my neighbors cultivates a garden of ever-increasing beauty, and another makes more and more noise, neither my increasing appreciation of the one nor my growing annoyance with the other comes to the attention of the Department of Commerce.'[66]

At the same time, economic growth involves a variety of indirect costs to society, such as 'the adjustment of social institutions' and of 'patterns of human life and work' that are inevitably influenced by the growth process. In 1962, Kuznets wrote prescient words:

> As a general formula, the desirability of as high and sustained a growth rate as is compatible with the costs that society is willing to bear is valid; but in using it to judge economic problems and policies, distinctions must be kept in mind between quantity and quality of growth, between its costs and return, and between the short and the long run.[67]

While national income did not account for pleasant non-monetary activities enjoyed by citizens, it fully included outlays and investment that may not be at all beneficial to society, at least in the long run. Having lived through two global conflicts and having actively contributed to the victory of the US against Nazi Germany, Kuznets was fully aware of how the invention of the national accounts had prompted military outlays and strengthened the military–industrial complex. As discussed in Chapter 1, he had supported the cause as he believed that succeeding in the war was 'at least equal in importance to the welfare of individuals'. But he was invariably convinced that – at least in ordinary times – 'no one would welcome an acceleration of the over-all rate of economic growth that was associated primarily with a marked increase in defence expenditures – at best a necessary evil, but still an evil'.[68] For some, the inclusion of defence spending into the GDP calculation was also problematic from a methodological point of view. If defence is a 'necessary regrettable' rather than a source of final utility to anyone (except, perhaps, soldiers and arms producers), then in the absence of serious external threats all defence spending could be eliminated and no one would be the worse.[69] Costa Rica, for instance, abolished the army in 1948 and there is no evidence that this has diminished the well-being of its citizens. To the contrary, it is the only country in the region that has not been involved in a civil war or suffered a coup since. By the same token, if defence spending is exclusively targeted at preserving the social and economic framework within which non-defence production occurs, then its value should already be incorporated in the market prices of civilian goods.[70] In this regard, adding defence spending as an additional component of GDP would result in an undue duplication. Moreover, analysts of the politics of national defence (which often revolves around the existence and maintenance costs of obsolete military bases) have long demonstrated that at least a substantial portion of defence spending makes no contribution whatsoever to national security.[71]

Many events and social transformations that are negative and detrimental to society can be hugely beneficial to GDP growth. Post-war reconstruction was a powerful boost for economic growth in the 1950s. Various types of natural disasters can also support GDP, at least in the recovery phase, when houses and infrastructure must be rebuilt, as was the case with Hurricane Katrina in 2005.[72] The same applies to social phenomena. Chris Eigel, executive vice president of Koenig & Strey, a large realty firm in suburban Chicago, once said: 'Unfortunately, divorce is a big part of our business. It means one [home] to sell and sometimes two to buy.'[73]

According to political economist Albert Hirschmann, industrial progress and economic growth were already 'viewed as an all-conquering, irresistible force'[74] long before the invention of GDP. All spheres of social life, from the family to the state, from traditional hierarchy to long-time cooperative arrangements, were being vitally affected by economic growth: metaphors often used to describe this action ranged from the outright 'dissolving' to 'erosion', 'corrosion', 'contamination', 'penetration', and 'intrusion' by the 'juggernaut market'.[75]

In the 1970s, economist Fred Hirsch dealt at length with what he called 'the depleting moral legacy' and the 'social limits' of GDP growth. He also introduced the concept of 'defensive expenditures'; that is, what people have to spend to protect themselves against the social and environmental degradation caused by economic growth.[76] According to his research, important resources for welfare such as the social climate, the quality of human relationships and the capacity for collective cooperation seem negatively correlated with growth: 'As individual behaviour has been increasingly directed to individual advantage, habits and instincts based on communal attitudes and objectives have lost out.'[77] Since traditional cultures are often an obstacle to GDP growth, their destruction and substitution with a system favourable to growth is a necessary condition for the latter to come about. Throughout history, when cultural and social characteristics proved sufficiently resilient to the direct permeation of market principles, governments were called upon to use their political and administrative leverage to foster growth goals. In the seventeenth and eighteenth centuries, the enclosure of communal lands in Great Britain was a paradigmatic case of government-led policy to push for economic growth. It indeed brought about a collapse of free consumption and monetized the exploitation of natural resources, thus constituting a precondition for the formation of an industrial labour supply. In *The Great Transformation*, the political economist Karl Polanyi paralleled the process of human and natural resource exploitation that characterized the establishment of 'market society' in modern Europe with the treatment reserved to traditional institutions in the colonies at the beginning of the twentieth century.[78] Others pointed out convincingly the instrumental role played by governments in using GDP targets (often with the support of international financial institutions such as the International Monetary Fund and the World Bank) to open up space for capitalist markets in traditional societies, while some have more recently shown the effects of the 'shock doctrine' to impose structural reforms and liberalize economies during and after major disasters.[79]

According to Hirsch and his followers, GDP growth is driven by its own destructive power. It can only sustain itself through the destruction of non-market goods, as it is endogenously fuelled by a decrease in free consumptions that must be substituted with costly ones.[80] Public parks and squares, beaches and lakes, as well as communal pastures, do not add to GDP unless their usage is somehow restricted and monetized. The paradigmatic example of this situation is urban living. Cities are places built for work, where low-cost opportunities are rare, beginning with the scarcity of places where people can meet. From the point of view of leisure, most cities offer a wide variety of costly entertainment (e.g. theatres, cinemas, stadiums, etc.), while free consumption is hard to find. Moreover, in a city, individual welfare often depends on what others do, given that people are closely interdependent and the negative impact of economic activities on common resources tends to be higher than elsewhere. This is what Italian economists Antoci and Bartolini call the 'air conditioner syndrome'. By taking the city of Tokyo as an example, they argue that the widespread use of these devices, which cool the interior of buildings but emit heat to the exterior, forces more and more city dwellers to buy air conditioners, thus generating a vicious circle of 'defensive

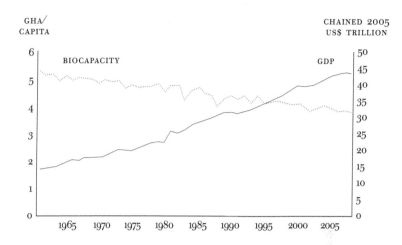

GHA/
CAPITA

CHAINED 2005
US$ TRILLION

FIGURE 2.2   Global GDP growth financed by spending down
the world's natural wealth

Source: *Beyond GDP: New Measures for a New Economy* (Demos: New York 2012).

consumption'. GDP growth becomes a self-reinforcing process in so far as it produces negative externalities that, in turn, force people to further contribute to growth.[81]

As already pointed out by Nordhaus and Tobin in the early 1970s, there are some socially productive assets (for example, the environment) that do not appear in any GDP balance sheets. Their services to producers and consumers are not valued in calculating national income. By the same token, no allowance is made for the depletion of their capacity to yield services in the future. The prevailing standard model of growth assumes that there are no limits to the feasibility of expanding the supplies of non-human agents of production. It is basically a two-factor model in which production depends only on labour and reproducible capital: 'Land and resources, the third member of the classical triad, have generally been dropped.'[82] Quite worrisomely, though, these simplifications of the theoretical conceptualization of GDP carried over not only into empirical work but also into policymaking. For many politicians and their economic advisers, capital and technology are a near-perfect substitute for land and other exhaustible resources: 'If substitution for natural resources is not possible in any given technology, or if a particular resource is exhausted, we tacitly assume that ... innovations will overcome the scarcity.'[83]

According to the World Resources Institute, the systematic neglect of resource depletion in national accounts has long generated a number of 'illusions', especially in those nations whose GDP growth depends heavily on natural resource exploitation.[84] Net product and net capital formation are overestimated. Fiscal deficits of central governments that own natural resource enterprises are underestimated. Current account deficits in a nation's balance of payments may be masked by unsustainable sales of natural assets. These statistical distortions encourage a policy of excessive reliance on short-term natural asset depreciation, with serious consequences for future environmental sustainability. The inverse relationship between GDP growth and natural resources is clearly illustrated in Figure 2.2, where the upward curve of global GDP is compared to the downward trend in biocapacity.

In 1972, a book titled *The Limits to Growth* provided the first systematic account of the potentially irreversible damage provoked by continuous GDP growth. The study, conducted by a team of researchers of the Massachusetts Institute of Technology through a pioneering use of computers to build future scenarios and simulations[85] – a level of sophistication unparalleled at the time – was commissioned by a group of intellectuals known as the Club of Rome, an international committee of distinguished business people, state officials and scientists founded by Aurelio Peccei, an Italian industrialist and public intellectual. A core thesis of the study was that material consumption and pollution cannot continue forever in a finite world. Although human nature leads people to presume innocently that growth rates are linear, the ecological constraints of our planet and the scarcity of natural resources may easily trigger uncontrollable processes. The book then postulated that a continuation of the exponential growth of GDP as seen until the 1970s (with its industrial output, natural resource consumption and pollution) would inexorably widen the gap between the rich and the poor nations of the world and ultimately result in major global shortages by 2050 to 2070.[86]

The study came as a cold shower at a time in which the world had known more than two decades of unabated growth (and GDP euphoria) since the end of the Second World War. The moon had been conquered in 1969, nuclear energy was on the rise and there were no hints that mineral resources may one day run out. Its findings spurred significant interest and millions of copies were sold, especially when the 1973 oil crisis appeared to confirm the worries put forward by the authors. Arguably the most important contribution of the book was that it brought the critique of GDP outside of expert circles, thereby popularizing decades of concerns and scholarly debates about the long-term effects of economic growth. And it was perhaps for this reason that it was fiercely criticized from different angles, not only within the academic community but also, and more importantly, by opinion leaders and policymakers. Its conclusions were discredited as old-fashion Malthusianism, after the British political economist Thomas Malthus, who, in the early 1800s, had advocated in favour of, among other things, birth control, abortion and war to curb population growth and diminish per capita consumption. The report's main recommendation, which focused on the need to reduce GDP growth, was very unwelcome to those who had a large stake in the status quo. At the financial and industrial level, it challenged widespread commercial interests. At the political level, it scared governments, which feared dwindling tax revenue for public spending. Among professional mainstream economists, who had never addressed the question of how to plan for a steady-state economy, the book was seen as a threat to their dominance in advising on economic matters.[87] Among the most vigorous critics of the report were radical free-market economist Julian Simon and futurist Herman Kahn, who charged that such forecasts had 'been damned as foolishness or fraud by every serious economic critic'.[88] Indeed, some Nobel laureates in economics, namely William Nordhaus and Gunnar Myrdal, also criticized the study but their critiques were mainly aimed at the methodology employed rather than at its overall findings.[89]

In a way reminiscent of the stir caused by the projections of the Intergovernmental Panel on Climate Change, which made headlines over the course of 2009, *The Limits to Growth* was dissected and every minor incongruence pointed out to discredit it in the eyes of the public. Its forecasting models were seized upon by environmental sceptics, who dismissed them as a hysterical doomsday prophecy. Among other things, they argued that the book did not give enough credit to human ingenuity and adaptability, which would eventually find creative ways to replace depleted assets.[90] In addition, free-market economists claimed that the market mechanism, by adjusting prices accordingly, would lead to substitutions for scarce resources and would prompt inventors and entrepreneurs to develop various technological solutions, thereby preventing any collapse.[91] In 1989 Ronald Bailey, at the time science editor of the business magazine *Forbes*, published a sneering attack on the author of the report, whom he called Dr Doom, and on the book itself, which he considered 'as wrong-headed as it is possible to be'.[92] In 1993, he reiterated his accusations in a volume titled *Ecoscam*, and in 2002 in the book *Global Warming and Other Eco Myths: How the Environmental Movement Uses False Science to Scare Us to Death*.

In a discussion paper titled 'Malthus, Multinationals and the Club of Rome', Robert Golub and Joe Townsend of the University of Sussex accused the Club of Rome, which had sponsored the research, of conspiring to establish some 'kind of fanatical military dictatorship', which would rule the world and the economy at the service of multinational corporations. In their view,

> The Limits debate has already played a significant historical role in that it tended to confuse and demoralize public opinion (and perhaps even political leaders) so that there is now a fairly widespread feeling that the crises we face are qualitatively different from those of the past.[93]

According to Ugo Bardi, author of *The Limits to Growth Revisited*, it would have taken little effort to debunk most of these accusations. Yet, thanks to the support of certain media and the possible collusion of various industrial and economic circles, the smear campaign prevailed, and by the early 1990s, in spite of several reprints of the book, the issues raised by the study had become 'everyone's laughing stock'.[94] And it appeared of almost no relevance that William Nordhaus partly retracted some of his criticisms in a 1992 paper commissioned by the Brookings Institution, in which he argued that

> Economists have often belied their tradition as the dismal science by downplaying both earlier concerns about the limitations from exhaustible resources and the current alarm about potential environmental catastrophe. However, to dismiss today's ecological concerns out of hand would be reckless.[95]

In his reconstruction of how the study was 'demonized', Bardi draws a comparison with the case of the book *Silent Spring*, which in the 1960s unveiled the damaging effects of the use of DDT and other pesticides and marked a turning point in the evolution of environmental concerns in Western societies. The book and its author, the biologist Rachel Carson, were fiercely attacked by the chemical industry through a systematic strategy of professional and personal defamation involving lobbyists, business-friendly

media, a variety of pundits and a bunch of think-tanks funded by
the largest chemical corporations. By analogy, Bardi writes, one
could imagine that 'in some smoke filled room, representatives
of the world's industry had gathered to decide what measures to
take against [*Limits to Growth*] in order to bring the matter back
to proper perspective in the eyes of the public.'[96]

Although a number of think-tanks and political groups financed studies to discredit the findings of the study and the
concerns it raised for natural resources (among which the George
C. Marshall Institute and Competitive Enterprise Institute, ultimate bastions of scepticism-for-hire), the demolition of these
ideas over the course of the 1980s–1990s was more likely the
outcome of a spontaneous process, rather than an orchestrated
conspiracy.[97] The attractiveness of GDP growth and its promises
were perhaps too strong for most people to stop and reflect. For
the media, in particular, GDP served their deep cravings in so far
as it combined the appearance of empirical certitude and expert
authority with a ready-made story line. Moreover, it supported
the agenda of the industries that thrived on the kind of policies
it reinforced.

There is little doubt, indeed, that the popularity of national
income accounts has given the upper hand to all industries that
pollute and deplete, since GDP portrays these acts as economic
progress. This entrenched collusion between statistics and industrial interests came to light clearly in 1994, when the Clinton
administration proposed that resource depletion be subtracted
from GDP, following a suggestion from the Department of Commerce, increasingly influenced by decades of critical views coming
from progressive economists and the environmental movement.
In a critique of its own accounting practices, the Commerce
Department's Bureau of Economic Analysis pointed to several
'points of asymmetry' between its traditional treatment of natural
resources as opposed to that of infrastructure and industrial

equipment. As a remedy, they proposed to treat natural resources like business fixed assets and, by disaggregating the interactions between the economy and its natural environment, partly subtract their depletion from GDP.[98] Although the actual proposal put forward by government was in the end much more modest than what GDP critics demanded, at the House Appropriations Committee hearing in April 1994 various representatives from coal-rich states attacked the Department's staff and, after several delays and additional examinations, the proposal was dropped. As reported by Congressman Alan Mollohan, of West Virginia, if the national accounts were to include the depletion of coal reserves and the effects of air pollution, 'somebody is going to say ... that the coal industry isn't contributing anything to the country.'

What makes life worthwhile

In 1853, a journalist of the *Democratic Review* predicted that technological progress (at the time, mainly electricity and machinery) would transform life so much that by the end of that century 'Men and women will then have no harassing cares, or laborious duties to fulfill. Machinery will perform all work – automata will direct them. The only task of the human race will be to make love, study and be happy.'[99] Similarly, in 1930, Keynes predicted that, thanks to the increase in productivity, the average citizen in industrialized societies would work a maximum of fifteen hours per week by 2030.

Yet history had it otherwise. In the opening of her 1992 bestseller *The Overworked American*, sociologist Juliet Schor wrote:

> In the last twenty years, the amount of time Americans have
> spent at their jobs has risen steadily. Each year the change
> is small, amounting to about nine hours, or slightly more
> than one additional day of work. In any given year, such a

small increment has probably been imperceptible. But the accumulated increase over two decades is substantial. ... The rise of worktime was unexpected. For nearly a hundred years, hours had been declining. When this decline abruptly ended in the late 1940s, it marked the beginning of a new era in worktime.[100]

This has been the era of GDP. The era of the national accounts and infinite growth. The era of economic performance and sustained mass consumption. The era of greenhouse gases and climate change. The era in which economics took over all other social sciences to become the ancilla of power. During this period of time, economists have known very well that the maximization of GDP should not be a proper objective of policy, 'yet their everyday use of [it] as the standard measure of economic performance apparently conveys the impression that they are evangelistic worshippers'.[101]

Like Frankenstein in Mary Shelley's epic novel, Simon Kuznets recognized how dangerous his creature had become. Together with other far-sighted economists, some of them of Nobel fame and some less known, he tried to warn politicians and society about the potential manipulation and misconception surrounding GDP and economic growth. He continually repeated that it is nonsensical 'to urge that the overall growth rate be raised to x percent a year, without specifying the components of the product that should grow ... and the costs that may have to be incurred to assure such returns'.[102] He also realized that politicians looked at GDP growth as a response to immediate problems, which made them fundamentally blind to the long-term consequences of their actions:

If there are unused resources and groups in distress, the problem is immediate. On the other hand, the long run for the future is always uncertain. ... And yet ... public agencies are continuously making decisions that involve commitments for

THE FRANKENSTEIN SYNDROME

decades; and the policies directed at current problems all have long-term consequences.[103]

Yet, never mind how loud the chorus of GDP worshippers was, not everybody within the political arena was equally convinced by this almighty number. Probably the best known GDP sceptic among top-level politicians at that time was Robert Kennedy, who in 1968 ran for presidency on a platform of economic justice, racial equality, solidarity and demilitarization of the economy (he was a fervent activist against the Vietnam War). During his presidential campaign, in a historic speech delivered at the University of Kansas only three months before being assassinated, Kennedy spoke prophetic words:

> Too much and for too long, we seemed to have surrendered personal excellence and community values in the mere accumulation of material things. ... Gross National Product counts air pollution and cigarette advertising, and ambulances to clear our highways of carnage. It counts special locks for our doors and the jails for the people who break them. It counts the destruction of the redwood and the loss of our natural wonder in chaotic sprawl. It counts napalm and counts nuclear warheads and armored cars for the police to fight the riots in our cities. ... Yet the gross national product does not allow for the health of our children, the quality of their education or the joy of their play. It does not include the beauty of our poetry or the strength of our marriages, the intelligence of our public debate or the integrity of our public officials. It measures neither our wit nor our courage, neither our wisdom nor our learning, neither our compassion nor our devotion to our country, it measures everything in short, except that which makes life worthwhile.[104]

CHAPTER 3

The global quest to dethrone GDP

> Some of us have for a long time been pointing out the anomalies,
> perversities, and irrelevancies of GDP accounting. Like the
> citizens in a Chesterton story who petitioned the local magis-
> trate to close down a pub that served poisoned beer, our petition
> has met the official reply: 'Yes, the evidence supports your case,
> but before we sacrifice historical continuity by tearing down
> this admittedly noxious establishment, you must specify exactly
> what should be put in its place.'
>
> Herman Daly, author of *The Steady State Economy*

The Chesterton analogy is quite telling. Thousands of pages
filled with detailed accounts of the flaws of GDP as a measure of
economic performance (let alone as an indicator of welfare) were
not enough to convince politicians and mainstream economists to
stop using this indicator as a policy tool. 'No beer is better than
poisoned beer', argued the ecological economist Herman Daly,
one of the pioneers in the effort to rethink GDP.[1] Perhaps; but
people still wanted to get drunk. And for as long as the poisoned
beer was the only one available in town, then nobody would
question its bitter taste.

This is why, starting in the 1970s, a plethora of progressive economists, intellectuals, think-tanks, NGOs, foundations, governmental agencies as well as various types of civil society groups have attempted to 'dethrone' GDP by replacing it with a 'better' number. Some of these proposals have been rather formal, mainly aiming at polishing and smoothening GDP by deducting 'bads' and incorporating additional 'goods'. In this category, we find a long tradition of thought in economics seeking to improve GDP by adding measures of economic welfare and genuine progress. Championed by progressive ecological economists, these approaches have become rather common also among governmental institutions, especially the UN and the World Bank. More recently, new attempts have been made at going 'beyond' GDP. These calls focus on enlarging the set of available indicators, by adopting 'dashboards' rather than aggregate indexes, with a view to diluting the influence of GDP by providing a variety of additional and complementary measures of sustainability and well-being. Although useful, this approach does not call into question the underlying assumptions of GDP growth and its political agenda. Finally, some proposals have been more radical, disputing whether economic growth is an acceptable goal in its own right and arguing that, instead of trying to complement or improve GDP, policies should be based on a completely different understanding of well-being. Such reforms have been put forward mainly by civil society groups and environmentalist think-tanks, with the support of a handful of progressive governments.

This indefatigable production of alternative indicators has progressed in parallel with an international public debate characterized by heated confrontations regarding the scale and significance of environmental degradation and the policies needed to address it. In 1972, the United Nations Conference on the Human Environment (usually referred as the Stockholm Conference) marked the beginning of a long series of summits at the global

level and was accompanied by the unavoidable political battles
that have characterized environmental politics ever since. In
spite of mounting pressure exerted by environmental movements,
the interests of the US industrial lobbies (largely supported by
the personal intervention of the then secretary of state Henry
Kissinger) prevailed and, in the conference's final document,
delegates rejected the notion of sustainability, preferring the less
compelling expression 'eco-development'. It took another fifteen
years of negotiations and quibbles before the World Commission
on Environment and Development, better known as the Bruntland
Commission, finally introduced the official definition of sustainable development as 'development that meets the needs of the
present without compromising the ability of future generations
to meet their own needs'.[2] Its report, aptly titled *Our Common
Future*, was welcomed by the UN General Assembly with Resolution 42/187. In 1988, the Intergovernmental Panel on Climate
Change was established by the World Meteorological Organization and the United Nations Environment Programme, and later
endorsed by the UN through Resolution 43/53. Finally, two Earth
Summits, in Rio de Janeiro in 1992 and in Johannesburg in 2002,
marked the process that eventually led to the entry into force of
the Kyoto Protocol in 2005, currently the only existing global
agreement on climate change. Although playing a leading role
in the early negotiations under President Clinton, the US never
officially signed the protocol, which was actively opposed during
the two tenures of George W. Bush. In 2009, the UN Framework
Conference on Climate Change held in Copenhagen revealed the
growing resentment of developing countries vis-à-vis the West
for failing to recognize the broader social justice implications
of climate change. Emerging economies such as China, India,
Brazil and South Africa broke ranks, thus sinking hopes that a
new agreement would be reached any time soon. In 2011, under
the conservative leadership of prime minister Stephen Harper,

even a traditional supporter of global environmental legislation such as Canada pulled out of the Kyoto Protocol. In 2012, the Rio+20 summit marked two decades of summitry on sustainable development, and in the same year the Stockholm+40 conference took stock of all outstanding issues and problems identified by the international community with a view to upgrading the debate and relaunching systematic reforms in terms of economic and environmental governance.

The debate on alternative measures to GDP has mirrored the contradictions of the global debate on sustainability. Significant steps forward were taken in times of progressive environmental politics, almost invariably followed by setbacks and regressions as soon as more conventional economic concerns took centre stage. The next sections will discuss the tension between the attempts made at improving GDP as opposed to those aimed at replacing it, focusing in particular on the role of governmental institutions and on those individuals who challenged the politics of GDP and our societies' resistance to change.

Improving or replacing GDP? The search for alternative indicators

The first internationally renowned attempt at revising GDP was made by William Nordhaus and James Tobin in 1971, when they developed an index called Measure of Economic Welfare (MEW). In their calculations, these two Yale economists reclassified expenditures 'as consumption, investment and intermediate' in order to achieve a better distinction between final and non-final goods as Abramovitz had indicated (see Chapter 2).[3] Moreover, they took into account the views of those lamenting that a measure of welfare should also include the contribution of leisure and household work. Furthermore, recognizing the impact that the 'bads' associated with economic growth may have on welfare, they introduced a number of corrective parameters 'for some of the disamenities of urbanization'.[4] Quite importantly, they did not hesitate to exclude defence expenditures altogether. They saw no direct effect of defence expenditures on economic welfare. No reasonable country (or household), they argued, would buy national defence 'for its own sake'.[5] If there were no war or risk of war, there would be no need for defence expenditures and no one would be worse without them.

While proposing a better welfare measure, they nonetheless praised GDP as one of 'the economists' chief tools for short-run analysis, forecasting, and policy' and considered it important also for many other purposes.[6] Their MEW was therefore a re-arrangement of items of the national accounts to demonstrate that economic growth needed to remain a fundamental objective of policy, while a better understanding of welfare could be simply obtained with limited (largely technical) adjustments.

For most of the 1970s and 1980s, the economist Robert Eisner championed the call for a general reform of national account-ing in the US. His most well-known achievement in this field was the construction of the 'total incomes system of accounts' (TISA), which extended and revised official national income measures.[7] Among other things, TISA considered a large portion of government purchases (on roads, police, the military and the courts) as intermediate in nature and excluded them from the final output. Similarly, most work-related spending by households (e.g. commuting expenses) was subtracted as an intermediate cost of production rather than a source of consumer satisfaction. TISA also acknowledged the importance of non-market outputs, many of which are produced within the household sector. As a consequence, it incorporated the value of, among other things, meal preparation, house cleaning and painting, as well as care of the young and elderly.[8] According to Eisner's calculations, these various forms of household production exceeded – on average

– one-third of American GDP throughout the 1980s.[9] An additional issue raised by TISA was the fact that conventional GDP accounts excluded all tangible and intangible assets acquisitions by government and households, with the exception of new home purchases, thus assuming that only business undertakes all of society's investment activity. Through his recalculations, Eisner found that the reiterated claims made in the business press that the US government invested too little in the economy were grossly unfounded and that, by contrast, indiscriminate cuts in federal spending to eliminate the budget deficit could reduce public investment in transportation, education, new technologies and the like. In mid-2012, amid the endless debate on how to get the world out of the global economic downturn, the US Department of Commerce confirmed Eisner's concerns about the alleged proneness of business to spearhead society's investment in the economy: indeed, GDP growth projections needed to be revised downward because of plummeting investments in the private sector, in spite of skyrocketing profits accrued by most companies in the first quarter. The overall performance of the US economy was, once again, supported by households, which dipped into their savings, and got further indebted.[10]

Eisner's proposal helped deconstruct some 'myths' generated by the GDP mantra, in particular that 'business enterprises exist only to produce and invest on behalf of ultimate consumers' and that households are unproductive and their contribution is 'merely to enjoy commodities purchased from the business sector'.[11] At the same time, it failed to seriously rethink the GDP conceptual framework and its production-based paradigm. For instance, Eisner did not include the value of leisure time in his estimate of non-market output, ignored issues associated with employment (both the personal satisfaction of being productive and also dissatisfaction with poor working conditions) and neglected fundamental income distribution problems. Most importantly, the

TISA framework did not address concerns about depreciation of natural resources.[12]

The first coherent attempt at integrating macroeconomic, social and environmental data into a comprehensive measure of human welfare was carried out by the ecological economist Herman Daly and the theologian John Cobb in the late 1980s.[13] Daly and Cobb called their substitute for GDP the Index of Sustainable Economic Welfare (ISEW). It initially covered the period 1950–86. In the mid-1990s, it was renamed the Genuine Progress Index (GPI), with various updates computed until 2006. Acknowledging their intellectual debt to Nordhaus and Tobin, Daly and Cobb argued that it is the current flow of services to humanity from all sources, not just the output of marketable commodities, which is relevant to economic welfare. They also followed Abramovitz's reflection on the diminishing marginal utility of income and took into account the fact that 'an additional thousand dollars in income adds more to the welfare of a poor family than it does to a rich family.'[14] Hence, the greater the degree of income inequality, the lower the contribution to economic welfare. Following Eisner's calculations, they incorporated four 'service flows' that were generally omitted from official consumption measures: household labour, existing consumer durable stock, public streets and highways, and public spending on health and education.[15]

They also extended the range of defensive consumption by excluding most government expenses, household costs of commuting, insurances, pollution control, personal expenditures on education and medical care. An additional deduction from the welfare calculation was the cost of air, water and noise pollution. The depletion of natural assets was another set of concerns addressed by Daly and Cobb. They estimated and deducted the annual loss of productive services associated with the past and present conversion of wetlands and farmland to urban uses. They treated land development as irreversible and considered potential substitutes for the services of wetlands and farmland not readily available. Moreover, they believed that the marginal annual loss of benefits would rise with cumulative land conversion. As a consequence, their accounting methodology ensured escalating aggregate costs of land development as time unfolded. Extraction of non-renewable energy in the forms of oil, coal, natural gas and nuclear fuel was another category of natural capital depletion incorporated in the GPI. As they observed, 'depletion of nonrenewable resources ... [is] a cost borne by future generations that should be subtracted from (debited to) the capital account of the present generation.'[16]

Despite its roots in both economic theory and widely shared principles of sustainable development, the GPI was not without its detractors. Some conservative critics argued that it is incorrect 'to combine an indicator of current welfare with an indicator of sustainability' because costs associated with depletion of non-renewable resources and other forms of natural capital incurred by future generations make little difference to current welfare.[17] Other economic commentators pointed out that, in spite of its important contribution, the GPI remained a fundamentally arbitrary indicator with respect to what it included or implicitly excluded from the measurement of welfare.[18] For instance, while the GPI corrected for income inequality and natural resource depletion, it did not include corrections for the degree of political freedom or degree of equality between the sexes as if these elements were of no importance for personal and collective well-being.

Perhaps the most important theoretical (and also political) flaw of the GPI was that it assumed 'perfect substitutability among different forms of capital'.[19] The GPI was indeed one of the first attempts at 'monetizing' natural capital in an effort to incorporate it into the overall calculation of welfare. Natural resources were then measured according to their estimated economic value and their depletion subtracted from the contribution of other forms of capital. This monetization procedure invariably led to the paradoxical consequence that losses in terms of natural assets could be easily offset by equal or greater gains in terms of human-built capital. For example, if the value of a public park was set at $2 million (based on 'estimates' of how much it contributed to the well-being of residents), then its demolition could be neutralized if, in its stead, a school or a hospital of the same 'estimated' value were to be built. Animated by honest ecological concerns (and the legitimate conviction that what is not monetized is generally considered free or worthless), the approach of measuring all types of resources in terms of money has continued until the present day, producing all sorts of paradoxes and distortions.

Besides the GPI, a number of alternative indicators have been proposed throughout the years by a variety of think-tanks, investment funds, NGOs and foundations. Several efforts to measure not just the level of income but also how it is distributed and utilized were undertaken throughout the late 1970s and 1980s. Early social indicators in this regard included the Physical Quality of Life Index (PQLI) and the International Human Suffering Index (HSI). Published for the Overseas Development Council in the mid-1970s, the PQLI combined three basic indicators of well-being: infant mortality, life expectancy at the age of 1, and basic literacy. A more ambitious but perhaps less compelling effort to measure well-being was represented by the Human Suffering Index. Originally published by the Population Crisis Committee in 1987, the HSI used a set of ten – rather disparate – indicators to measure social well-being, including calorie supply per capita, access to drinking water, telephones per capita, political freedom and civil rights, inflation and GDP.[20]

Within this particular field, the civil society coalition Social Watch has been publishing a Basic Capabilities Index (BCI) since 2000, currently covering over 170 countries. Social Watch's approach rejects GDP as a measure of social development and, instead of measuring income, looks at 'different aspects of people's actual condition and their greater or lesser possibility of having their human rights fulfilled'.[21] The index consists of three indicators: the percentage of children reaching fifth grade, survival until the age of 5, and the percentage of births attended by skilled personnel. Precisely because it dispenses with income as an indicator, the BCI has proved to be highly correlated with measures of other human capabilities and, in particular, has shown a high degree of correlation with the indicators designed to track progress towards the Millennium Development Goals, the most far-reaching set of global standards sponsored by the UN. At the same time, its focus on 'capabilities' rather than on income has limited its popularity in more affluent societies. The Legatum Institute, a London-based think-tank connected to the Legatum investment group, has been publishing a Prosperity Index since 2007 with a coverage of 110 countries. This assessment, which is presented as 'the world's only global assessment of national prosperity based on both wealth and subjective well-being' includes various dimensions, from social capital to personal freedom and entrepreneurship.[22] Yet it also incorporates GDP as one of its key indicators.

On the environmental front, the best-known index is probably the ecological footprint, developed in the early 1990s by a Ph.D. student at the University of British Columbia, Mathis Wackernagel, currently president of the Global Footprint Network. The set of measurements (officially called national footprint accounts) was launched in 2003, with information drawn from the Food and Agriculture Organization, the UN Statistics Division, and the International Energy Agency, plus various studies published in peer-reviewed scientific journals.[23] The ecological footprint 'measures human appropriation of ecosystem products and services in terms of the amount of bioproductive land and sea area needed to supply these products and services'. In 2005, the network launched a lobbying campaign with the goal of institutionalizing the ecological footprint in at least ten key national governments by 2015. So far, more than twenty nations have completed reviews of the footprint, while only Japan, Switzerland, the United Arab Emirates, Ecuador, Finland, Scotland and Wales have formally adopted it. One of the major weaknesses of the ecological footprint is that data collection takes a significant amount of time and new information is often available only every two to three years.

The ecological footprint is an assessment of how many natural resources our economies use, but does not measure human well-being or economic welfare per se. An interesting attempt to combine measures of welfare with ecological impact is the Happy Planet Index developed by the UK-based New Economics Foundation in 2006 (and revised in 2009 with a coverage of 143 countries).[24] The index complements the ecological footprint with life satisfaction and life expectancy, thus rejecting income or GDP as a guiding parameter. It is an efficiency measure, in which the amount of well-being 'produced' is assessed against its environmental impact. Ever since its creation, the index has consistently shown that high levels of resource consumption do not produce comparable levels of well-being, and that it is possible to achieve high levels of satisfaction (as measured in conventional public opinion polls) without excessive consumption of the earth's natural capital. It has also emphasized that there are different routes to achieving comparable levels of well-being. In particular it has demonstrated that, while the model followed by the West can provide widespread longevity and variable life satisfaction, it does so only at a vast and ultimately counterproductive cost in terms of resource consumption. Interestingly, most Latin American countries have been consistently placed at the top end of the index's global ranking, led by Costa Rica: besides reporting the highest life satisfaction in the world, Costa Ricans also have one of the highest average life expectancy in the Americas (second only to Canada).[25]

Another interesting attempt stemming from a joint partnership between non-profits and legislative bodies is the platform called *The State of the USA*. Formally launched in 2007, but yet to become fully operational, this initiative aims to harness the power of the Web to allow American citizens to discover, understand and review hundreds of indicators on issues such as crime, energy, infrastructure, housing, health, education, environment and the economy. Besides a partnership with the National Academy of Sciences, which provides the methodological backing, and the support of various philanthropic foundations, *The State of the USA* has been boosted by the decision of the Obama administration to create a Key National Indicator System in 2010. In Canada, since the late 1990s, the Atkinson Charitable Foundation has sponsored a community-based process to define new indicators to measure the quality of life. In 2009, this effort resulted in the publication of the Canadian Index of Wellbeing and a number of associated reports.

Public institutions rethinking GDP?

Not only researchers, think-tanks and civil society groups have questioned GDP. Public agencies and governments have also promoted their fair share of revisionism, more often than not, though, without stepping out of their relative comfort zones. There is one notable exception: a small landlocked kingdom of a few hundred thousand souls, bordering the two most populous countries of the world, India and China.

The Kingdom of Bhutan introduced the concept of 'gross national happiness' (GNH) in 1972, when the new king Jigme

Singye Wangchuck, at the time aged 16, officially declared that his country would break away from a GDP-driven economic policy to adopt an approach based on Buddhist values. Although initially the move was simply rhetorical (with little or no real impact on statistical accounting), official policies began to take 'a holistic approach towards notions of progress and give equal importance to non-economic aspects of wellbeing'.[26] Traditionally, the concept of GNH was explained through four pillars: good governance, sustainable socio-economic development, cultural preservation and environmental conservation. It was only in 2005, though, that the government formally decided to develop GNH indicators. The Centre for Bhutan Studies was given the task of designing the methodology, and, after a number of consultations and local stakeholder meetings, the first GNH survey was carried out in a handful of districts in 2007. The four pillars were translated into nine measurable domains: psychological well-being, health, education, time use, cultural diversity, good governance, community vitality, ecological diversity, and living standards. A second (larger) survey was carried out in 2010, but its implementation took nearly nine months, a long time for a process that, ideally, should be conducted on a regular basis to inform ongoing national policies. Major stumbling blocks included the length of the questionnaires, the extensive fieldwork needed to reach the scattered population of some villages, and the sampling procedure adopted to ensure that respondents were representative of the national population (at district level as well as at the rural/urban level).[27]

Although it is best known as the first formal measure of 'happiness', the GNH is actually an assessment of 'sufficiency', in line with Buddhist ethics: according to its conceptual approach, a happy person is one who has enough of what he/she needs. This is why the survey does not include broad-brush questions on self-perceived happiness (something like 'taking all things together, would you say you are: very happy, rather happy, not very happy, or not happy at all?'). Rather, it focuses on a variety of carefully selected indicators, following the Alkire Foster method introduced by the University of Oxford to measure 'multidimensional' poverty.[28] Its scales do not range from 0 to infinite, but apply a 'cut-off point' based on sufficient level of achievement. In the case of living standards, for example, the sufficiency cut-off (which must always fall above the official poverty line) is the average of what is considered to be a 'good salary' by most respondents. When the achievements exceed the cut-off, they are replaced by the sufficiency level. Thus, if a respondent's actual income were 1,000 and the sufficiency cut-off were 150, then he or she would be treated as if earning 150.

Researchers at the Centre for Bhutan Studies are well aware that 'the level at which the sufficiency cutoff is set is a value judgment.'[29] They nevertheless argue that inevitable difficulties 'should not obscure the reasonableness of setting *some* sufficiency cutoff'.[30] In spite of the methodological problems that it may pose, this is arguably the most interesting contribution made by the GNH to the measurement of life satisfaction as it emphasizes that, beyond a certain point, the quality of life is no longer a mechanical process whereby individuals need only add new achievements to their 'shopping list' to live more happily. From a policy perspective, the focus on sufficiency forces government to place greater emphasis on supporting those who fall below the cut-off points rather than those who pass the threshold, given that any further improvements in the 'top' levels would not result in an increase in the final score. Addressing issues such as education, low living standards, community vitality and balanced use of time (which the survey has recorded as the most widespread of 'insufficiencies') has thus become a key objective of national policies.[31]

Granted, Bhutan only became a constitutional monarchy in 2008 and it remains a poor country, at least in conventional GDP terms. Moreover, its democratic credentials may be questionable, which begs the question of whose happiness or sufficiency is actually being measured.[32] Yet, the influence of its approach has grown over time. International conferences on gross national happiness have been held in Canada, Thailand and Brazil, and small to medium-sized projects aiming to measure national happiness at the local level have sprawled across the globe. In 2012, the non-profit *Gross National Happiness USA* was successful at convincing the government of Vermont to include a 'genuine progress' indicator to measure 'economic, environmental, and societal well-being as a supplement to the measurement derived from the gross state product and other existing statistical measurements'.[33]

Research conducted by the University of Leicester in 2006, based on data collected from a variety of sources, including the CIA, UNESCO, the World Health Organization and global opinion polls, found that Bhutanese people are among the most satisfied in the world.[34] The small Himalayan kingdom ranked number eight, right after prosperous countries such as Denmark, Sweden, Switzerland and Austria. By contrast, the US came only 23rd, the UK 41st and China 82nd. Bhutan was the only country in the top 20 with a low GDP record. In 2011, the UN General Assembly unanimously adopted a resolution, introduced by the Bhutanese government with support from another sixty-eight member states, calling for a 'holistic approach to development'.[35] This was followed in April 2012 by a UN High-Level Meeting on 'Happiness and Wellbeing: Defining a New Economic Paradigm' designed to bring together world leaders, experts, civil society and spiritual institutions to develop a new framework for global sustainability and well-being.

Also the World Bank has tried to complement GDP in an effort to step up its professed fight against global poverty. The first set of complementary indicators was introduced in 1978, after the then president, Robert McNamara, realized that, despite the 'unprecedented change' and 'impressive record' of economic growth in the previous quarter of a century, roughly half the world's population continued to be trapped in 'absolute poverty'. As a firm believer in the wonders of economic growth, he stated that the Bank would need new instruments to achieve the 'twin objectives' of development: 'to accelerate economic growth and to reduce poverty'.[36] The premiss that economic growth and poverty reduction are 'inextricably linked', although not logically equivalent, led the Bank to expand the set of basic development indicators. By the early 1980s, the list had evolved into a different set of six variables: population, area, per capita GDP, life expectancy, adult illiteracy rate, and inflation rate. Although the list of additional indicators has been growing ever since, one should not overestimate the Bank's commitment to a multidimensional view of economic development. Its economists acknowledged that GDP 'does not, by itself, constitute or measure welfare or success in development', but they continued to employ it as 'the main criterion used to classify economies and broadly distinguish different stages of economic development'.[37]

In the past decade, the Bank has also introduced new measures of 'total wealth', drawing inspiration from 'the ideas of the classical economists, who viewed land, labor, and produced capital as the primary factors of production'. One of the key indicators employed in these studies is the so-called adjusted net saving, better known as genuine saving, which purports to be a measure of sustainability by looking at how much countries provide for the future.[38] As a saving estimate, it calculates the amount of GDP that is not immediately used for consumption, to which it adds the investment in human capital minus the depletion of natural resources.

Total wealth indicators distinguish between produced capital (including the sum of machinery, equipment, infrastructure and urban land), natural capital (including land resources, forests and sub-soil assets) and intangible capital (a wide array of assets such as human capital, quality of institutions and governance). Given the scope of the data collection, the gathering is quite cumbersome, so total wealth estimates are only published every five years. In the latest report, titled *Where is the Wealth of Nations? Measuring Capital for the 21st Century*, the Bank convincingly demonstrated how relying solely on GDP would result in distorted estimates of national wealth. Specifically, it concluded that 'in all countries, intangible capital is, by far, the largest share of wealth' and 'in poorer countries, natural capital is more important than produced capital', thus suggesting that properly managing natural resources should become a fundamental component of development strategies, 'particularly since the poorest households in those countries are usually the most dependent on these resources'.[39] In a suggestive simulation, the report concluded that if resource-dependent economies had consistently invested the equivalent value of the natural resources depleted in the production process from 1970 to 2000, they would have substantially increased their overall wealth. For instance, a major oil exporter such as Nigeria could have had a stock of produced capital five times higher. Similarly, Venezuela could have four times as much produced capital. In terms of per capita GDP, Venezuela, Trinidad and Tobago, and Gabon, all rich in petroleum, could have reached a level of produced capital comparable to that of contemporary South Korea.

Probably the best-known attempt to challenge the hegemony of GDP in national accounting was made by the UN Development Programme when, in 1990, it introduced the Human Development Index (HDI). The underlying assumption of the HDI is that people 'are the real wealth of a nation' and that the basic objective of development is to create 'an enabling environment for people to enjoy long, healthy, and creative lives'.[40] As opposed to GDP, the HDI 'emphasizes sufficiency rather than satiety' and views the expansion of national income as a means to promoting human development, not as an end in itself.[41] In this case income is regarded as a necessary but not sufficient condition to achieve human development, which must be complemented by two additional dimensions: health (based on life expectancy) and education (based on school enrolment). Recognizing that low incomes typically satisfy basic needs whereas high incomes are spent in part on luxuries, the HDI uses a deflated version of per capita GDP to take account of the declining contribution of higher income to human development, with very little weight attributed to increases in GDP per capita above the world median.

The theories put forward by Indian economist and Nobel laureate Amartya Sen, which emphasize individual capabilities as a key component of human development, were instrumental in the methodological construction of the HDI. It is not by chance that the first scientific director of the *Human Development Report*, the Pakistani economist Mahbub ul Haq, was one of Sen's old acquaintances from college. As Sen recalled in an interview with the *New York Times*, 'many of our professors at Cambridge suggested that if a country could increase its GDP, then all the good things would follow. But that seemed to both Mahbub and me to be wrong.'[42] Their argument was not against GDP per se, but rather against the mainstream approach of relying 'only on GDP'. Almost forty years later, when Haq asked Sen to help him devise the HDI formula in 1990, Sen recoiled at the idea. 'I told Mahbub that it's vulgar to capture in one number an extremely complex story, just as GDP is vulgar.' But Mahbub called him back and said: 'Amartya, you're exactly right. What I want you to do is produce an index as vulgar as GDP but more relevant to our own lives.'

Ever since its creation, the HDI has been widely used by scholars, intergovernmental institutions and international donors, especially in the less affluent nations of the world. Yet it has not managed to make significant inroads in the policymaking community, let alone replace GDP. For some, the index provides a skewed understanding of human development given that it adopts socio-economic indicators but excludes measures of political freedom and human rights.[43] Over the years, this had generated evident paradoxes, including the fact that Egypt, Libya and Tunisia, the three countries swept by the popular uprisings of the Arab Spring in 2011, were consistently ranked at the top of the African continent, with scores that approximated those of the most industrialized nations. The HDI has also been considered of little use for more affluent countries, as their scores scarcely differ from one another. Indeed, most of these nations enjoy nearly universal adult literacy, and the transformation procedure for income levels essentially equalizes their per capita GDP data.

Moreover, many American economists and policymakers have criticized the HDI because it has consistently ranked the US below some European countries, thus casting doubts on the 'Stars and Stripes' development model. As testily argued by the libertarian economist Bryan Caplan, 'Scandinavia comes out on top according to the HDI because the HDI is basically a measure of how Scandinavian your country is.'[44]

Over the course of time, the HDI has been modified several times and since 2010 has introduced a new inequality-adjusted score which is supposed to indicate the 'actual level of human development', while the original HDI can be viewed as 'an index of the potential human development that could be achieved if there is no inequality'.[45] Then, in 2012, the UNDP launched the idea of a 'sustainable' HDI to take into account the cost of human development for future generations.[46] Sen himself has recognized that there are much better survey data now than when the HDI was developed. Moreover, problems associated with social and environmental phenomena such as migration, urbanization and climate change (which are completely excluded from the HDI) have become more pressing. Thus, in order to provide a more comprehensive blueprint for national account-ing better suited to deal with new challenges, Sen accepted the invitation to become part of a special commission set up by Nobel laureate Joseph Stiglitz and French economist Jean-Paul Fitoussi in 2009 upon request of the then president of France, Nicolas Sarkozy. Although the group gave itself the convoluted name of Commission on the Measurement of Economic Performance and Social Progress, its actual objective was to identify alternative measures that policymakers could use to replace GDP. In its final report, the Commission recommended broadening the spectrum of information regularly published by national statistical offices so as to include measures of health, education, political par-ticipation and governance, social connections and relationships, environment and insecurity (of both an economic and a physical nature). It did not go as far as to say that statisticians should also measure happiness, but it remarked that 'objective and subjective dimensions of well-being are both important' and specific surveys should be introduced to capture people's life evaluations.[47] With respect to sustainability measures, the Commission advocated combining physical indicators of climate-change-related phenom-ena (such as the atmospheric concentration of greenhouse gases) with conventional economic models converting all natural assets into a monetary equivalent. Nonetheless, they acknowledged that such a 'monetizing' approach has 'several limitations, the most important being the absence of many markets on which valuation of assets could be based'. Moreover, even 'when there are market values, there is no guarantee that they adequately reflect how the different assets matter for future well-being.'[48]

In conclusion, the Commission warned against the temptation of combining all these measures into one single aggregate number. Rather, it proposed the concept of 'dashboard' and used the metaphor of a car driver to justify it. GDP is one single dial, which tells you how fast you are going. But any reasonable driver (read our policymakers) would also want to know how much fuel is left, how far can the car still go and the overall mileage covered so far.

> [A] meter that added up in one single number the current speed of the vehicle and the remaining level of gasoline would not be of any help to the driver. Both pieces of information are critical and need to be displayed in distinct, clearly visible areas of the dashboard.[49]

Following the recommendations put forward by the Stiglitz–Sen–Fitoussi commission, the OECD published the report *How's Life?* in 2011, which looked 'at the most important aspects that shape people's lives and well-being', including housing, health, work and life-balance, education, social connections, civic engagement and governance, environment, personal security and subjective well-being.[50] Moreover, it created an interesting interactive tool known as Your Better Life Index, which allows users not only to assess the performance of countries based on various dimensions of well-being, but also to set the weight (that is, the importance) that each dimension has on the final score. Its slogan is 'there is more to life than the cold numbers of GDP and economic statistics.'[51]

Also the European Union and some Western countries have taken the cue from the Commission's work. For instance, in France, Germany, the UK and the US, governments have set up specific task forces to look at new indicators to complement GDP. Indeed, the 'dashboard' approach has had significant appeal across the policy spectrum, most probably because it poses fewer political concerns than an outright substitution of GDP. Indeed, adding a few more 'dials' to the system of national accounts may require some additional financial resources but it does not imply a whole paradigm shift. There is, indeed, a lesson that can be drawn from the myriad attempts to replace GDP as the leading indicator of our societies: it is one thing to devise, recommend and implement new indicators; it is another to overcome the political and economic interests that do not want to let go of GDP.

Resistance to change

According to Stiglitz, President Sarkozy was sincere in his attempt to find alternative (and better) measures to GDP. 'What he said was that he felt this tension: he is told to maximize GDP but he also knows as a good politician that what people care about are things like pollution and many other dimensions to the quality of life', Stiglitz reported to the *New York Times* in 2010. 'When he comes up for election, people are going to grade him on GDP, but people are also going to grade on the quality of life. And so he sort of said: Can't you in some way resolve this tension by constructing measures that don't pose these dichotomies?'[52]

According to the US deputy secretary of commerce, Rebecca Blank, new national measures depend not only on new statistical formulae but also on better cooperation across statistical agencies and additional financial resources. And, most importantly, political willingness. She was not averse to some of the Commission's recommendations (in particular she endorsed the idea of including a household perspective in the US national accounts), but pointed out that the time may not be ripe yet for major revisions: in some cases we know what should be done but 'don't have the money to do it'; in others 'we need to collect additional data that we don't currently have'; and in some other instances 'we don't really know how to do it quite yet'.[53]

As discussed in Chapter 2, the Department of Commerce proposed discounting resource depletion from GDP back in the mid-1990s, but the proposal met with the resistance of Congress. According to Geoffrey Heal, an expert on valuing ecosystem services and an adviser on green growth to the World Bank, it would only take a few months for a country to include resource depletion in the national accounts. Yet a unilateral move is quite unlikely and significant progress would only be achieved if the world's developed nations agreed to do it together. At the same time, a full system of environmental accounting still poses serious methodological challenges from an economic point of view. 'We can put monetary values on mineral stocks, fisheries and even forests, perhaps. ... But it's hard to put a monetary value on alteration of the climate system, loss of species and the consequences that might come from those.'[54]

A revision of economic measures is also likely to affect the credibility and reputation of many leading nations in the world. According to the OECD, for instance, if household production and services were to be included in official estimates, the US economy would be surpassed by a number of European countries in terms of GDP growth rates, thus shaking deep-seated convictions behind the American economic dream.[55] Interestingly, an inclusion of the household economy would also change general perceptions surrounding the economic downturn in Europe. For instance, two 'battered' economies such as Portugal and Spain would see their economic indicators reverse from negative to positive, as households' activities account for about 50 per cent of the economy in these nations. Although formal, this shift would have an important political impact: it would signal the end of the economic recession in both countries.

A lingering question is whether some governments, perceiving dangers in a new measurement system, might conclude that such an overhaul would wreak political havoc and therefore ought to be avoided. A telling example in this regard is the controversy surrounding the introduction of the green GDP in China. In 2004, the Chinese government announced that a 'green' index, which deducted the cost of environmental damage and resources consumption from GDP, would become China's main measure of economic performance.[56] At that time, the Asian giant was on the rise in the international arena, and the bid for the 2008 Olympics (a symbolic triumph for China's soft power) was strengthened by reassurance that environmental quality would be taken seriously by government.

Pan Yue, the young and dynamic deputy head of the State Environmental Protection Administration (SEPA) (upgraded to the status of Ministry of Environmental Protection in 2008) was the early champion of the initiative and managed to win the tacit support of the Party's bigwigs in Beijing. Since no other country had ever developed a comprehensive methodology to estimate the full environmental costs to be deducted from GDP, Chinese authorities decided to set up the system from scratch and invited local government authorities to cooperate. The process was divided into three sequences: the calculation of the natural resources consumed in economic activities; the assessment of environmental loss caused by economic development; and the monetization of the quantity of resources and environmental loss. For over two years, the technical team conducted accounting analysis on physical quantification of environmental pollution and imputed environmental degradation cost for forty-two industrial districts and three regions in East, Central and West China.

Published in 2006 (but with data from 2004), the first report showed that the economic loss caused by pollution amounted to 511.8 billion yuan ($66.3 billion), equivalent to 3.05 per cent of the national economy. Of the figure, environmental costs by water pollution, air pollution, solid wastes and pollution accidents accounted for 55.9 per cent, 42.9 per cent and 1.2 per cent of the total costs.[57] Even the National Bureau of Statistics, which led the data-gathering process in spite of its notorious reluctance to revise economic growth figures, affirmed that the green GDP can help people understand the hidden costs of development, urging them to realize that 'it is unreasonable to purely seek economic growth while ignoring the importance of the resources and environment.'[58]

Proudly, Yue declared that this work marked 'only the beginning of our efforts in a Green GDP calculation'.[59] In spite of his enthusiasm, though, the green GDP project was buried right after the publication of its first report. Methodological problems, political tensions and economic interests ended up derailing the initiative. For starters, the official authorities of the regions with a lot of polluting industries – such as Ningxia, Hebei, Shanxi and Inner Mongolia – refused to cooperate in data collection. Many local government officials feared that the green GDP initiative would turn into a naming and shaming exercise. Actually, Yue had made no secret that the new metric could be used to rank officials by their 'greenness' and punish those with a bad track record. However, this approach ran counter to a decades-long tradition within the state apparatus, which based promotion for officials on the economic growth rate of their localities.

Moreover, SEPA and the National Bureau of Statistics began bickering over methodology and funding, and tensions intensified ahead of the 17th National Congress of the Communist Party held in October 2006.[60] SEPA publicly admitted that the study, although shocking to many Chinese officials, only reported conservative estimates. This was due to the fact that the National Bureau of Statistics had relied exclusively on basic data and rudimentary techniques, thus focusing only on the cost of environmental pollution, without accounts of natural resources depletion and ecological damage. 'On the whole,' SEPA admitted, 'this accounting result is only a fraction of ultimate green GDP.'[61]

Yue publicly denounced highly polluting industries and their connections with segments of the political establishment. In order to conduct proper environmental assessments, he ordered the closure of thirty construction sites worth over $14 billion, including some projects associated with the controversial Three Gorges Dam, the world's largest power station, which has caused the displacement of 1.3 million people since 2005. Moreover, green GDP team leader Wang Jinnan accused local governments and the statistical agency of foot-dragging. Finally, when the National Bureau of Statistics pulled out of the initiative in 2007, the project languished and the next year's report was postponed indefinitely.[62]

Although the green GDP project galvanized some like-minded provincial leaders (especially in those modest-sized cities where green industries have been taking root) and forced the Party Congress to place greater emphasis on sustainable development and environmental protection, the country's leaders continue to fear 'that going too green too fast' may hurt their business partners and their political clout, both domestically and internationally.[63] In the meantime, Yue continues his battle for a more sustainable Chinese economy, and his new position as deputy minister increases his leverage. In an interview with the British magazine the *New Statesman*, which nominated him Person of the Year in 2007, Yue described his country's economic performance in the following terms: 'This miracle will end soon because the environment can no longer keep pace.' And, based on his estimates that environmental damage has cost China 8 to 15 per cent of GDP per year (well beyond the official green GDP estimates of 2006), he concluded 'that China has lost almost everything it has gained since the late 1970s due to pollution'.[64]

The resilience of GDP was also evident in early 2012, when a furious controversy was stirred by President Obama's decision to nominate Dr Jim Yong Kim, a renowned physician and academic, for the presidency of the World Bank. Dr Kim came under fire when the media found that, in a book titled *Dying For Growth: Global Inequality and the Health of the Poor* published a decade earlier, he had written that

The idea that robust economic growth will automatically lead to a better life for everybody is comforting. Unfortunately, it is also wrong. ... [The] quest for growth in GDP and corporate profits has in fact worsened the lives of millions of women and men.[65]

The reactions by mainstream economists, free-market magazines, pro-growth opinion leaders and conservative bloggers were fierce. *The Economist*, for instance, wrote a scathing attack on Kim's nomination, favouring the appointment of orthodox economist Okonjo-Iweala, Nigeria's finance minister. It blamed Kim for quoting radical activist Noam Chomsky in his books and for praising Cuba's health policies. 'Were Mr Kim hoping to lead Occupy Wall Street, such views would be unremarkable', added the magazine. But the Bank 'promotes growth because growth helps the poor. If Mr Kim disagrees, he should stick to medicine'.[66] Quoted in the *Financial Times*, New York University economist and staunch defender of free-market economy William Easterly referred to Kim as 'the first World Bank president ever who seems to be anti-growth', when 'even the severest of World Bank critics like me think that economic growth is what we want'.[67] A headline on the website of conservative policy advocate David Horowitz read: 'Obama's pick for World Bank hates capitalism', while a spate of economic policy blogs depicted Kim as a 'Castro-type commie'. Finally, the online magazine of the American Enterprise Institute maintained that 'to put someone in charge of the World Bank in 2012 who holds a fundamental misunderstanding of what creates economic growth and how nations escape poverty would be a disaster in both political and human terms.'[68]

Needless to say, Kim was forced to review his opinion on GDP growth. He went on a so-called 'global listening tour' to solicit inputs and priorities from heads of state, finance ministers and other experts. When he returned, he penned an op-ed for the *Financial Times*, in which he wrote that 'today more people live in fast-growing economies than at any time in history' and that 'development can take root anywhere'. Importantly, integration with the global economy 'can transform a poor country into one of the most dynamic and prosperous economies in the world'. And he concluded: 'I recognise that economic growth is vital to generate resources for investment in health, education and public goods.'[69] On 16 April 2012, Dr Kim was elected president of the World Bank.

GDP strikes back

The first version of the United Nations System of National Accounts (UNSNA), which is the international standard for GDP statistics managed by the UN Statistical Commission, was published in 1953. As discussed in Chapter 1, it drew extensively on the pivotal research conducted in the US by Kuznets and his colleagues. Over time, the system was reformed according to the evolutions of the market economy and the specific interests of participating states. In 1968, the UNSNA went through a partial reform aimed at further developing some of its key concepts, in particular the distinction between market and non-market production, the classification systems, the statistical units and the boundary of assets that are seen as adding to national income. After this reform process, Japan and Australia joined in and, in 1970, the then European Community adopted some of its components.

As countries began to develop their own national accounts, the statistical community went on refining the underpinnings of the system. As discussed at length in Chapter 1, the end of the Cold War marked a fundamental turning point in the history of the national accounts, consolidating the authority of GDP as 'the only game in town'. The countries of the former socialist bloc abandoned what was then known as the System of Balances of the National Economy (a conventional standard uniting all economies that utilized the material product as opposed to GDP) and joined in the global club. In the meantime, the globalization of markets forced statisticians to keep up with the evolution of complex economic and financial mechanisms.

These shifts in the world's political and economic arena led to a major revision of the UNSNA in the late 1980s to early 1990s, with new guidelines being published in 1993.[70] At that time, the concerns of environmental movements that GDP failed to account for the depletion of natural resources and the consequences of environmental degradation had made some inroads among UN statisticians. The outcome of this revision process was not to revise GDP, as most progressive economists and environmentalists had hoped, but rather to create the so-called system of satellite accounts, a parallel set of calculations incorporating, among other things, indicators to gauge the scope of the informal sector and consumption of environmental resources. Ever since, the use of satellite accounts has allowed focusing on 'new' issues without affecting the comparability of the central framework used for economic policymaking.

The UN reviewers rejected the call for an outright revision of GDP because of their reluctance to add any further imputations to the national accounts. In their motivations, they criticized environmental advocates for trying to impose 'normative measures'.[71] They also believed that, since natural resources are not 'purchased' from Mother Nature, whatever valuation one may come up with would inevitably be artificial and controversial. Hence, better no valuation at all than a distorted one. They also distinguished between depletion (of natural resources) and depreciation (of man-made assets): unlike the first, the second refers to consumption of goods 'whose production has already been fully accounted for in the system'.[72] By contrast statisticians do not recognize nature as a factor of production, and therefore its provision of resources (and the depletion thereof) cannot be recorded in the accounts, which makes the SNA framework unsuitable for environmental accounting.

After the 2002 conference of the International Association of Official Statistics, which was devoted to the theme 'Official Statistics and the New Economy', the OECD encouraged its partner organizations, from the UN Statistical Commission to EUROSTAT, the World Bank and the IMF, to embark on an update of the 1993 SNA. The new set of revisions was officially published in 2008 and the most important changes regarded the financial sector, which had become one of the key drivers of GDP growth. A first reform regarded the computation of pension expenditures, which saw the introduction of new systems to take into account the diversification of pension schemes among public and private suppliers. Moreover, due to the mounting pressure of policymakers and brokers, the financial assets boundary was expanded to include also financial derivative contracts, a burgeoning industry of speculation that would soon cause the entire global economic system to plummet. Finally, the 'apparent' wealth produced by financial speculation (against which Kuznets had warned in the early days of the national accounts) was fully integrated into GDP accounting so as to become a key driver of measured economic growth.

In this new version, the UNSNA came to include all production actually destined for the market, whether for sale or barter, but it kept on excluding production of services for own final consumption within households (except for the services produced by paid domestic staff and imputed rental of owner-occupied dwellings). Similarly, no estimate was included for labour services of individuals provided without cost to non-profit institutions (e.g. volunteering). The revision process reaffirmed the principle that a 'necessary condition' for an activity to be treated as productive is that 'it must be carried out under the instigation, control and responsibility of some institutional unit that exercises ownership rights over whatever is produced'.[73] For example, the natural growth of stocks of fish in the high seas not subject to international quotas is not counted as production, given that the process is not managed by any proprietary institution and the fish do not belong to any organization or company. By contrast, the growth of fish in fish farms is treated as a process of production and therefore adds to GDP. Similarly, the natural growth of wild, uncultivated forests or wild fruits or berries is not counted as production, whereas the cultivation of crop-bearing trees, or trees grown for timber or other uses, is counted in the same way as the growing of annual crops. However, the 'deliberate felling of trees in wild forests', and 'the gathering of wild fruit or berries, and also firewood' count as production.[74] Following the same logic, rainfall and the flow of water down natural watercourses are *not* processes of production, whereas storing water in reservoirs or dams and the piping or carrying of water from one location to another *all* constitute a positive increment to national income.

The 2008 revision did not limit itself to closing the door to an incorporation of environmental costs into the calculation of national income. It also rehashed an old concern of progressive economists: that is, the computation of military expenses as part of GDP. Up until then, expenses on offensive weapons (such as bombs, torpedoes and spare parts) were only included as part of national income for the period of acquisition, regardless of the length of their life. This meant that weapons could be sold or exported in another accounting period, thus producing counter-intuitive entries in the accounts for government. In order to resolve this merely technical inconsistency, the 2008 revision recommended that *all* military expenditure on items used for a period longer than a year must be treated as capital formation, thus contributing fully to the calculation of GDP. The 2008 revision also eliminated the 1993 requirement to differentiate between expenditures on military 'assets' that could be used for civilian purposes (which are recorded as capital formation) from those that cannot (which count as expenditure).

It is hard to say whether specific pressure was made by arms-producing countries to have this reform introduced. Needless to say, this hardly noticed statistical 'adjustment' had significant implication for their total GDP given that global expenditures and sales of weaponry make up one of the largest markets in the world. According to the Swedish research institute SIPRI, since the 1990s global military expenditure by governments has regularly grown, totalling $1,738 billion in 2011.[75] The huge economic weight represented by military spending has been constantly paralleled by the profits of arms-producing companies, most of which are concentrated in the US and Western Europe. According to SIPRI, the top hundred arms-producing companies made profits of over $411 billion in 2010, with over 60 per cent of the sales being accounted for by US-based companies. In line with their GDP growth, emerging powers such as China, India and Russia have become the biggest investors in military equipment after the US, accounting for about 15 per cent of global spending.

Poisonous beer

Alternative indicators have played an important role in sustaining and strengthening the critique of GDP. In many cases they have provided much needed meat to be added to the bones of the intellectual and philosophical struggle to reconsider GDP growth as the guiding principle in contemporary societies. At the same time, it would be incorrect to argue that all alternative indicators aimed at the same goal. Most attempts, especially those carried out by public institutions, did not call into question the main tenets of GDP growth. As remarked by Alex Michalos, a senior adviser to the Canadian Index of Wellbeing, the main barrier to producing real change has been that statistical agencies around the world are run by economists and statisticians: 'And they are not people who are comfortable with human beings.'[76]

For most Western governments, for instance, measuring well-being (or happiness, as it has become fashionable to refer to it these days) appears more like a smokescreen exercise to 'humanize' statistical accounting, without any real grip on policy. For instance, the widely heralded measurement of happiness spearheaded by UK prime minister David Cameron in 2011 has been – so far – limited to the inclusion in existing household surveys of very generic questions such as: 'How satisfied are you with your life nowadays?' 'To what extent do you feel the things in your life are worthwhile?' 'How happy/anxious did you feel yesterday?'[77] But, as argued by the New Economics Foundation and the UK Centre for Well Being, well-being is more complicated than this and needs to be handled in a more nuanced way if policy is to be based on it.[78]

In many respects, the new stress on well-being remains superficial and is not necessary leading to a deep reconsideration of GDP growth as the quintessential parameter of success. As admitted by David Cameron in his well-known 'happiness speech' of November 2010,

> growth is the essential foundation of all our aspirations. ...
> [W]e are doing everything possible to try and drive a new economic dynamism in our country. We're trying to make it easier for people to start their own business, we're cutting corporation tax, we're getting behind entrepreneurs. ... [And] we'll continue to measure GDP as we have always done.[79]

The initiative launched by the UK Conservative Party, and arguably all similar initiatives presently under way in some Western governments, remain a far cry from the example of Bhutan. By introducing additional indicators, they have mainly tried to 'complement' GDP in an effort to make economic growth 'look' more sustainable. The underlying assumption of most of these attempts has been that GDP growth and negative externalities can be somehow 'decoupled': if GDP gets cleaned up bit, then the economy would be able to continue operating 'business as usual' without major consequences for the environment and society. This process, which, paraphrasing Herman Daly, could be defined as the 'angelization of GDP', has been more pervasive than one would think, providing most of the intellectual support to the much-talked idea of 'green' growth.[80] In Britain, the Lib-Dem leader Nick Clegg has been toying with the idea of introducing a so-called 'GDP+' by 2020, so as to incorporate the value of ecosystems into national wealth.[81] Since 2010, the UN has been working on an 'inclusive wealth' indicator designed to capture the economic value of human, social and natural assets and combine it with produced capital into one single number. Launched at the Rio+20 summit in 2012 with the coverage of twenty countries, this new indicator only marginally altered the historic patterns marked by GDP, showing that – when non-production assets are taken into account – overall growth rates tend to be lower for most countries, including emerging economies.[82]

The various forms of 'green' accounting and the creation of satellite accounts, which collect data on several aspects of economic and social life (e.g. the environment, tourism, unpaid household work), have marked an important step towards a more comprehensive system of national statistics. In many cases they have helped public opinion recognize some of the contradictions of economic growth and have provided environmental groups with additional data to advance their goals. At the same time, satellite systems remain fundamentally distinct from the central accounts used to measure national income. At best they constitute a 'side dish', while the media hunger is all focused on GDP as the main course.

Moreover, most of these 'new' measurements have ended up relying on the very same approach used by GDP to monetize the intrinsic value of assets, with an additional complication: as market prices for social and environmental resources are not available in real life, they need to be 'invented'. As a consequence, the market mentality has expanded its reach. Its valuation procedures have come to govern not only conventional goods but also the vast realm of intangibles that make up social and natural capital. And a flurry of 'price tagging' has ensued, as economists and statisticians nowadays apply cost–benefit analyses and opportunity costs to the monetization of virtually anything. So-called environmentally adjusted net domestic products and valuation methods for ecosystem services are being presented at international conferences and development summits. In 2010, the World Bank launched the 'Wealth Accounting and Valuation of Ecosystem Services', a global partnership to build consensus and work towards a common methodology to measure the economic value of natural resources.[83] Meanwhile, just like the burgeoning offset industry in the field of climate change mitigation, natural capital accounting is becoming a new business for many consultancies, private firms, investment groups and the like.

It must be recognized that most of these initiatives are genuine in their ultimate goal. They are honestly trying to use economic reasoning for the preservation of social and environmental quality. In their view, pricing would force people into 'a rational decision-making frame of mind' to analyse the 'gains and losses' of a certain type of developmental trajectory.[84] This 'frame of mind' implicitly assumes that the price of social and natural resources can always be measured. Generally, the methodology used is based on the so-called 'willingness to pay' principle: the price of ecosystems (which cannot be purchased in the market) is considered equivalent to the maximum amount a person would be willing to pay, exchange or sacrifice in order to preserve it. But in a society characterized by consumption frenzy and designed to underestimate the value of social and natural assets, how could the willingness to pay be a reliable parameter? Moreover, nothing can have an 'infinite value' and prices invariably lead people to think that commodities are exchangeable. As a consequence, the depletion of natural resources can be offset by, for instance, an equivalent investment in other fields. The removal of a park to build a kindergarten would result in a perfectly balanced sheet, with no negative impact on sustainable development or, in economic terms, with a net opportunity cost for future generations equivalent to zero. In this type of accounting, what we take away from nature is rebalanced by what we invest in human development. Prices create the illusion that natural goods and services can be exchanged on the market as if they are conventional factors of production. The natural sciences' concept of 'strong sustainability' – that is, the idea that certain resources are scarce and irreplaceable and therefore human activities must be subjected to the limitations of the planet's capacity – has been gradually substituted by the economic principle of 'weak sustainability', which holds that any type of capital is perfectly substitutable for natural capital as an input to production.[85]

At the Rio+20 summit in June 2012, a bunch of financial institutions (including some of the world's most powerful investment and commercial banks) signed a 'natural capital declaration', in which they pledged to integrate environmental accounting into their financial operations. In their own words, 'every economic activity can have an impact on natural capital. ... These impacts can lead to material financial risks, but also to relevant business opportunities.'[86] Reacting against the growing excitement surrounding the monetization of ecosystem services, the environmental advocacy group Greenpeace pointed out that giving numerical values to 'deeply interconnected natural systems is inherently speculative and not always sensible.'[87] Aggregated indicators can be dangerously misleading as they ignore 'the interconnectedness of natural systems' and the 'possibility of tipping points and abrupt changes'. Moreover, they give the impression that humankind can control nature as 'assets' so as to have a possibility to 'bail out' earth systems when they break down. But the earth is not a financial market and if we ignore planetary boundaries 'a bail out may be too late, and no money in the world will be able to help us'. This is why one needs to be very careful about what is being measured and for what purpose, what can be controlled and what cannot. And 'when we're leaving out invaluables from calculations, it doesn't mean that they are ignored, it means that they are paid special attention.' Putting a price on ecosystems may force us recognize the economic contribution of nature. Yet, it may also open up dangerous possibilities for a marketization of natural resources, given that anything that has a price can be bought and sold.

As already pointed out by E.F. Schumacher in the 1970s, 'to measure the unmeasurable is absurd and constitutes but an elaborate method of moving from preconceived notions to foregone conclusions':

> The logical absurdity, however, is not the greatest fault of the undertaking: what is worse, and destructive of civilisation, is the pretence that everything has a price or, in other words, that money is the highest of all values.[88]

In the end, in spite of tons of alternative numbers, GDP is still alive and well. Worse: its way of thinking has permeated other sectors and most well-meaning attempts at finding alternative measures. Apparently, poisonous beer is harder to let go of than many would have thought.

CHAPTER 4

Change from below

I don't believe that the solutions in society will come from
the left or the right or the north or the south. ... This is how
change will appear: you won't notice the difference. It won't be
anyone winning over anyone. It will just spread. ... It will be so
natural. It will be something that the intelligent people do.

Karl-Henrik Robèrt, founder of *The Natural Step*

It was at the end of 2001 when the system collapsed. By then,
the Argentinian government had tried all possible avenues to
regain investors' confidence in an effort to prop up its economy.
It had bowed to the diktats of financial markets and had followed
the IMF's instructions slavishly. It had implemented a series of
unprecedented austerity measures and curtailed public spending. Retirement benefits had been slashed and working hours
increased. Yet, unemployment stood at 20 per cent and social
discontent was on the rise. Hundreds of supermarkets were shut
down after looters broke in and emptied shelves. Angry citizens
struck out against banks, businesses and multinational corporations. Confrontations with armed police officers became a daily
occurrence, especially when the *cacerolazo* movement, after the

people who banged *cacerolas* (stew pots) to call for attention, took to the streets of Buenos Aires.

The rating agency Standard & Poors placed Argentina on credit watch. In a wave of collective hysteria, millions of citizens began withdrawing money from their accounts and sent all their savings abroad. In response, the state froze bank accounts and capped the sums of cash available to account-holders. A few weeks later, following the collapse of the currency, the government was forced to default on its debt obligations. Soon, there was no cash at all circulating within the economy.

Bartering began to rise spontaneously in communities, especially on the outskirts of Buenos Aires and in rural areas.[1] It was a completely new experience for many Argentinians. Although a *red de trueque* (bartering network) had been created by a small group of farmers in the early 1980s, few people had any prior knowledge of barter markets, and initially groups of citizens simply showed up at public spaces such as schools, parks and churches.[2] They brought used clothes, home-made food and other items with a view to exchanging them. It soon became apparent that communities characterized by higher degrees of local production in value-added areas such as food and clothing had a strong advantage vis-à-vis those that had traditionally relied on large retailing services and imported goods.[3] The collapse of the conventional economy also revealed a stark contrast between urban and rural areas. In cities, most bartering dealt in used and second-hand goods such as clothing and furniture as well as services, including healthcare. In spite of their initial reluctance, even nurses and doctors agreed to provide their services in exchange for various types of material goods.[4] Nonetheless, a significant portion of the urban population had nothing or little to offer and resorted to scavenging in waste and recycling scraps. In contrast, most rural areas began to prosper as they found new and better ways to produce a diverse range of durable goods and, in particular, food. Local markets where farmers could sell their produce mushroomed across the country, more often than not thanks to the introduction of community-managed local currencies alternative to the official peso, the most widespread of which being the *credito*.[5]

The breakdown of imposed societal norms, which often led to chaos in cities, actually helped bring about a cultural renaissance in many parts of the countryside. As new forms of production and consumption took root, communities began to reorganize economic processes from below. Closed-down factories were repossessed by retrenched workers, who started running them as co-operatives, as exemplified by the movement of *fabricas recuperadas*.[6] New emphasis was also placed on direct participation. Collective decisions, whether in factories or in local markets, were generally based on consensus. Voting was considered a last resort, only to be used when unanimity could not be achieved. Despite inevitable complications and latent tensions, these initiatives aimed to foster participation by all strata of society with a view to safeguarding the basic needs of every individual and, most importantly, avoiding social and political exclusion. The preservation of cohesion was considered more important than decisional efficiency, as long meetings and strenuous deliberations became quite common.[7]

Although labour-intensive services were in greater demand, intellectual and artistic work was not abandoned. Indeed, markets and other community events presented opportunities for information and cultural exchange. Music, street theatre and various other types of arts served not only as entertainment but also as outlets for public protest and resistance. Murals on public buildings and highways often reflected local communities' struggles against the political elite and large industries.

Needless to say, the shift from an economy of mass consumption to a localized system of self-production was not without some hiccups. For instance, the boom in local currencies combined with a decrease in production led to inflation. This became particularly noticeable when one needed to replace items not manufactured locally. As a consequence, services fared best in areas where they were run by local co-operatives, whose members had a strong interest in maintaining a balance between their economic activities and the community's needs. As rules regarding property rights became more relaxed, squatter camps popped up in many peripheral areas of the major cities, often causing distress and conflicts.

Eventually, the conventional economy got back onto its feet. The political class was reshuffled and new leaders emerged. In spite of lofty rhetorical remarks about alternative economic plans, GDP growth was reaffirmed as the chief objective of national macroeconomic policy. Several barter markets were undermined by official authorities and sabotaged by corporate interests.[8] In many areas of the country, especially in the major cities, the system went back to business as usual. Or did it? As a matter of fact, pockets of resistance remained active throughout the nation. Indeed, the crisis had brought about a fundamental opening. It had shown that an alternative economic system was possible, and that citizens could take the lead in reshaping the economy – and, as a consequence, democracy – from below.

Ever since the mid-2000s, and in particular with the outbreak of the Great Recession, similar experiences have mushroomed throughout the world, especially in Europe. Climate change and the financial crisis have forced hundreds of thousands of people to call into question the conventional economy. As macroeconomic policies have continued unaltered despite the evident threats posed by environmental degradation and financial instability, citizens have decided to take matters into their own hands and have launched a wealth of grassroots initiatives. Most of them have never reached a significant critical mass and remained confined to a specific territory. Others have been absorbed into more conventional non-profit and third-sector activities, thus losing their innovative character and becoming part and parcel of the more traditional social economy. In some cases, though, the systematic effort to challenge the politics of GDP has given birth to fully fledged movements spanning countries and continents. This chapter discusses some interesting examples of how civil society has been rethinking the pillars of mainstream economics: that is, how we produce, how we consume and the role of money.

In transition to a 'degrowth' society

In the early 2000s, Rob Hopkins was a teacher at the college of further education in Kinsale, a town of about 7,000 people in West Cork, Ireland. Hopkins focused on permaculture: that is, an approach to ecological design and agricultural systems centred on natural ecosystems.[9] Not only was his course the first-ever full-time module entirely dedicated to this new discipline, but it was also deeply focused on building practical knowledge: the emphasis was 'on giving students a toolkit that they can use in their lives to make their homes, their communities and their world more abundant and sustainable'.[10] Over time, students learned the principles and applications of permaculture by building straw-bale houses, putting up polytunnels, planting forest gardens, digging ponds and erecting dry-stone walls. Then, in 2005, they got imaginative. They used their theoretical and practical experience to draft an 'energy descent' action plan for their town, in which they proposed a detailed road map to help transition towards a low-energy-consumption future.[11]

Shortly thereafter, Hopkins moved to Totnes, a small town in South West England, where he joined forces with other activists to found the first transition initiative in the world.[12] At the beginning, Transition Town Totnes (TTT) consisted of a handful of committed volunteers devoting their spare time to the practice of permaculture. As part of their voluntary work, Hopkins and his fellows also ran awareness-raising events in the district, which exposed them to other communities sharing similar concerns about economic imbalances, environmental degradation and the depletion of natural resources. In late 2006, at an early UK transition meeting held in Bristol, a fortunate encounter with the foundation Tudor Trust allowed the TTT founders, in partnership with others, to secure initial funding to launch a network. They opened an office, hired a small core team of staff, put together a 'wiki' website and published the handouts of their workshops, collated in the first edition of a Transition Initiatives Primer. In late 2007, the Transition Network began its training activities with a first intake of eighteen people. Meanwhile, Hopkins went back to his desk and completed the *Transition Handbook*, which was finally published in 2008 and sold over 25,000 copies.[13]

Since those early days, the project has grown remarkably. Their training programme has spanned the world, having been replicated in a number of countries and regions. Currently there are hundreds of people involved in some capacity in TTT and more than thirty running projects, some implemented in collaboration with local authorities. Essentially, TTT is now an umbrella organization made up of various groups and clusters focusing on a wide variety of activities, from education programmes to renewable energy projects, from health and well-being to building and housing.[14] Companies such as the Totnes Sustainable Construction Company and the Totnes Renewable Energy Society Ltd have been created to oversee the building of sustainable infrastructure and facilitate the diffusion of community-generated renewable energy projects. Community projects have been put forward to turn abandoned industrial sites into offices for eco-friendly businesses and public spaces, all equipped with renewable energy sources.[15] When TTT was chosen as one the projects to be awarded funding by the UK Department of Energy and Climate Change, grants were made available for the systematic installation of photovoltaic panels across the town. The project was named 'Transition Streets' and the grant, over half a million pounds, was part of a government initiative known as Low Carbon Communities Challenge.

The transition 'philosophy' has been largely influenced by concerns regarding the consequences that a peak oil scenario would have on society at large. Ever since Shell Oil Company researcher Marion King Hubbert developed his 'peak theory' in the 1950s, most experts have agreed that the amount of petroleum under the ground in any region of the world tends to decline over time.[16] Therefore the rate of discovery increases when new fields are identified but, following a bell-shaped curve, it invariably drops over time. According to the US Energy Information Administration, the production of crude oil in America peaked in the 1970s and has steadily declined since.[17] At the global level, although the International Energy Agency had initially projected a consistent growth in crude oil production, in its 2010 World Energy Outlook it had to revise such optimistic predictions. Taking into account political factors and investment bottlenecks, the agency concluded that the world had already reached its 'peak' in 2006 and projected a descending curve for the coming decades.[18]

The very idea of 'transition' stems from the recognition that 'the real problem is not to imagine a future without oil, but to find practical ways to get there'.[19] In this view, what really matters is the process; that is, the sequence of fundamental steps that will allow societies to transition to a more sustainable future. Moreover, the concept of transition gives the sense that 'we are not going backward': as a word, 'it identifies the opportunity in what we can all do together'. All transition initiatives (which in the meantime have spread to include not just 'towns', but also villages as well as urban neighbourhoods in major cities and districts) focus on drastically reducing human dependence on fossil fuels in an effort to diminish environmental degradation and curb climate change. At the same time, they aim to make communities more resilient and adaptable to the shifts required by a low carbon economy while strengthening civic participation, solidarity and social cohesion. Starting from a realization that the GDP development model is humanly and ecologically not sustainable as it causes irreparable damage to our ecosystems and living environment, the transition initiatives have become laboratories of alternative economic thinking and practice. In doing so, they are also experimenting with new forms of democracy. They are entirely founded on principles of bottom-up self-organization and encourage collective decision-making on public goods, thus challenging the power of technocrats that thrive under the GDP paradigm. They promote self-governance and espouse many tenets of deliberative democracy, whereby each resident-member is encouraged to contribute towards collective decisions affecting the management of common resources.

A special emphasis is placed on public goods such as food and energy. These initiatives strive to identify new and better ways to produce food locally in order to privilege grassroots knowledge and expertise, while reducing food miles that push up prices and damage the environment. In all the projects, a fundamental goal is to avoid long supply chains, promote local ownership and encourage reusing and recycling. Jobs such as cobblers and grinders, traditionally endangered by the 'buy new' philosophy underpinning GDP, as well as local craft markets, where people can sell a variety of home-made products, have re-emerged in the communities joining the movement. The same principles have also been applied to the production of energy. Indeed, transition initiatives have fundamentally reinterpreted the use of renewable sources with a double goal: replace fossil fuels and encourage sharing. Unlike fossil-fuelled energy, which is highly centralized and can only be generated on a massive scale, renewable energies are suitable for small-scale locally owned projects, which strengthen the autonomy and resilience of communities vis-à-vis industrial interests. Moreover, they promote a different understanding of common goods based on cooperation rather than competition. As a consequence, energy is not simply produced locally: it is 'co-produced' through specific collaborative schemes, whereby community members cooperate (and invest) in the installation of common solar panels and wind turbines while sharing the energy produced therein.[20] Most of this infrastructure is self-built rather than purchased from renewable energy corporations, thus further increasing the autonomy, know-how and resilience of local communities. The emphasis on self-production and self-consumption, sharing, recycling and reusing is viewed in fundamental opposition to the GDP model of consumption, which requires things to be purchased, burned up, replaced and discarded at an ever-accelerating rate. While the GDP mantra encourages societal 'obesity', the transition movement promotes a culture of healthy food. Moreover, the focus on resilience and durability (of goods as well as of community infrastructure) challenges the built-in obsolescence of market products, which are often scientifically 'designed' to break, given that continuous replacement is the ultimate weapon of consumerism.[21]

As of 2012, the registry of the Transition Network boasted about 1,000 entries corresponding to an equal number of initiatives across over thirty countries, mostly in Europe and South America, but increasingly also in North America, Africa, Oceania and Asia. According to their website, these initiatives 'are actively and cooperatively creating happier, fairer and stronger communities, places that work for the people living in them and are far better suited to dealing with the shocks that will accompany our economic and energy challenges'. Fully aware of the rate at which the transition philosophy is spreading across the world, they ambitiously regard themselves as a 'social experiment on a massive scale'.[22] On the same day as the Rio+20 Earth Summit in June 2012, the network and its partners organized a 'festival of transition', inviting people across the world to challenge the GDP system by simply carrying out 'uneconomic' activities such as spending time with family and friends, going for a walk, joining other neighbours in the community and, above all, speaking about climate change and how simple citizens can organize to stop it.

The transition philosophy has gained popularity also in the US, where recent trends suggest that social and cultural change at the local level is occurring in spite of timid leadership from government (barring, perhaps, the First Lady's efforts to popularize gardening and fight obesity).[23] For example, since the 2008 financial meltdown, grassroots food co-operatives have expanded to work with people receiving federal government assistance. Moreover, community gardens have popped up in a number of cities, small communities have advanced renewable energy projects, and low-carbon approaches have affected lifestyles and collective action. According to Transition US, there are over one hundred initiatives throughout the country that, in one way or another, subscribe to the transition approach. In 2011, they launched an initiative to support the installation of home and community gardens throughout the nation, which was modelled on the experience of the 'victory gardens' popularized during the Second World War to reduce the pressure on the public food supply and boost local resilience. During a May weekend, more than 1,500 big and small initiatives were officially documented in over 200 cities, with hundreds of families and community groups using their own private yards or reappropriating oft-abandoned communal gardens to grow vegetables, plant trees and build ecological housing.

Furthermore, many community co-operatives, local farms and community-supported agriculture farms have made healthy local food choices available to the most nutritionally at-risk and economically disadvantaged, in an attempt to address the shortage of quality food available to many citizens. Indeed, land-use policies designed to support GDP growth mainly through investment in massive housing projects have facilitated the emergence of segregated neighbourhoods, where most basic services are scarce and food security has become a significant problem. In these areas, the presence of grocery stores is limited (or non-existent) due to low profitability, as the poor have less money to spend on healthful and nutritious food, which in turn has generated 'food deserts' where malnutrition and a number or diet-related conditions are spreading.

One critical issue the movement is still grappling with is how to connect grassroots activism with advocacy activities. Campaigns have been carried out in favour of innovative projects, but seldom against specific interests, whether of governmental or corporate nature. 'Transition doesn't dictate anything. We try to talk to everybody, from the business community to political leaders.'[24] When they run campaigns, they concentrate on the local dimension, where divergences can often be resolved without conflict. 'We may rally the community against the building of a new chain store, but would not campaign against an existing local business. We pick our battles very carefully.' So far, transition initiatives have refrained from getting involved in the political terrain, mainly for fear of losing the broad support they enjoy among different types of people. They feel that endorsing an explicit political 'manifesto' may push supporters away while reducing the capacity of the movement to bridge divides between different values and cultures. Their pragmatic, non-ideological stance, coupled with their reluctance to engage in explicit advocacy work, has, in some cases, elicited lukewarm reactions from more radical environmental movements, which would expect the transition initiatives to be outspoken in favour of social justice and against capitalist interests. In a 2008 pamphlet titled *The Rocky Road to a Real Transition*, some critics from the left attacked the apolitical character of the transition culture: 'How can we talk about climate change and peak oil and not deal with politics or side with the communities struggling against the expansion of fossil fuel infrastructure?'[25] Ever since, there has been an ongoing debate within the movement with respect to striking the right balance between politics, advocacy and community work.[26] In many regards, transition is something that 'sits alongside and complements' the more militant culture of environmental movements. For its founders, one reason why the transition philosophy is growing so fast 'is precisely because it is addressing and responding to the very real concerns people feel about rising fuel costs and the changing climate without polarising people'.[27]

Because of their ambition to rethink the conventional economic paradigm, the transition initiatives can be considered a practical example of 'degrowth': that is, 'a downscaling of production and consumption that increases human well-being and enhances ecological conditions and equity on the planet'.[28] Although some of the tenets of degrowth can be found in most cultures and philosophical traditions (as the concept relates intimately to values such as modesty and frugality), the first scientific works on the subject were only carried out in the 1970s in the aftermath of the publication of *The Limits to Growth* (see Chapter 2). The country where this approach found the most fertile terrain was France, where the word *décroissance* was introduced by the followers of the Romanian American economist Nicholas Georgescu-Roegen, one of the intellectual forefathers of ecological economics. In the 1970s, Georgescu postulated that economic processes follow the same entropy law as physical processes and, by applying the second law of thermodynamics to economics,

concluded that human economic activity flourishes at the expense
of ecosystems by consuming free energy in transformations and
exchange of resources, goods and services.[29] Hence the impossibility of infinite growth in a finite world. With a view to relating
economics to the limits of the biosphere, he then advocated for
the replacement of traditional economic science with what he
called 'bioeconomics'.

It was only in 2002, though, that the concept of *décroissance*
began to attain some popularity among opinion leaders, when
the ecologist magazine *Silence* devoted an entire special issue to
the theme and the UNESCO headquarters in Paris hosted an
international conference titled *Défaire le développement, refaire
le monde* ('Unmake development, remake the world'). In Italy, a
civil society alliance to promote *decrescita* was created in 2004
and more initiatives followed a few years thereafter. In Spain,
the words *decrecimiento* and *decreixement* (in Catalan) became
increasingly popular as of 2006. The English term 'degrowth' was
formally adopted at the first official conference of the movement
held in Paris in 2008, which also marked the commencement
of systematic academic research in the field as well as advocacy
campaigns carried out by international civil society groups. Ever
since, biannual conferences of the movement have been held in
Barcelona (2010) and in Venice (2012).

Unlike the transition movement, most degrowth initiatives
have been led by intellectuals animated by an explicitly political
and advocacy thrust. Degrowth promoters call for a future where
societies live within their ecological means, with open, localized
economies and resources more equally distributed through new
forms of democratic institution. They do not advocate for merely
negative GDP rates, as they appreciate that pure, unmanaged degrowth (such as that experienced during an economic recession)
has negative repercussions on society while producing little or no
improvement for the environment. According to York University

economist Peter Victor, there is no escape from the fact that ecological limits impose some degree of contraction on the world's
economic systems. However, there are at least two different ways
in which this can be achieved: by 'disaster', as is the case with
recurrent crises (never mind if caused by imbalances in supply
and demand or by the scarcity of resources) or by 'design', through
specific long-term policies aimed at sustaining an equitable transition to a low-intensity economy.[30] The Great Recession triggered
by the global economic crisis is an example of exogenous degrowth
by 'disaster', as it is imposed on societies by the collapse of the
financial system. By contrast, degrowth promoters believe in an
endogenous contraction by 'design': through a set of voluntary
and coordinated macro- and micro-level policies. As part of their
political agenda, they argue that GDP should be dismissed as
'an overarching policy objective' in order for society to focus on
alternative patterns of production and consumption fully compatible with the limits of the ecosystems. Considering the addiction
to GDP growth as 'humanity's cancer', they are fully aware that
political reforms may not be enough if they are not supported
by a comprehensive cultural revolution aimed at rethinking the
ultimate values and goals of contemporary societies.[31]

Degrowth is regularly criticized by opinion-makers and mainstream political parties. Critics on the right argue that it would
plunge the world into chaos, while those on the left see it as a
luxury that only the wealthy bourgeoisie can afford. By contrast,
defenders take pains to explain that degrowth is not just a project
for environmental sustainability but also an action plan for social
justice. In their view, degrowth is not a glorification of the des-
titution and inequalities of a wretched past or a romanticized
return to the Stone Age. Much to the contrary, they view it as
a blueprint for the future and recognize that, given the cultural
permeation of GDP growth within contemporary societies, a shift
will only be possible through a good degree of 'decolonization of

the imaginary'.[32] Thus, degrowth aims to develop a new language by which to redefine what we mean by progress.

In the words of Serge Latouche, arguably the most prominent intellectual within the movement, a degrowth society can be built through the realization of 'virtuous circles' represented by eight 'Rs': *re-evaluate* our societal values in order to give primacy to cooperation vis-à-vis competition, altruism vis-à-vis egotism, the pleasure of leisure vis-à-vis the obsession with work; *redefine* concepts such as poverty and wealth as well as scarcity and abundance by breaking free from conventional economic categories, which have led to the privatization and marketization of natural resources; *restructure* the productive apparatus in order to make it compatible with a paradigm shift; *redistribute* resources by using ecological footprints as a benchmark of equity within nations and across countries; *relocalize* production systems and decision-making authority in order to build strong and participating local communities; *reduce* the impact of consumption and production on the biosphere; fight the built-in obsolescence of conventional market products by *recycling* what cannot be *reused* directly.[33]

Similar to the transition initiatives, degrowth societies are described as hubs of innovation where human ingenuity is targeted at identifying new social and technical arrangements that will enable people to live convivially and frugally. The shrinking of the GDP economy is viewed as a necessary step to leave more space for human cooperation and eco-friendly practices. The local (and rural) dimension of life, largely marginalized by the urbanization processes triggered by economic growth, is reinterpreted as the pillar upon which to found these new societies. In their new language, degrowth promoters speak of 'grassroots postmodernism', 'economunicipalism', self-organized 'bioregions' and 'ecopolis'.[34] They imagine networks of villages rather than cities, where new forms of local 'ecological democracy' are practised. They are undoubtedly influenced by the history of Italian communes in the Middle Ages and the lessons of republicanism, with its strong emphasis on civic participation. They cite Hannah Arendt's principles of *vita activa* and propose governance reforms that are reminiscent of William Weston's recountals of *Ecotopia* in Ernest Callenbach's best-selling novel.

There are also important differences between the two approaches, especially at the conceptual level. While degrowth argues that GDP growth is not only unsustainable but also inherently unethical, the transition philosophy aims to build a post-growth society 'out of necessity', mainly because of the energy and climate crises.[35] In the first case, there is a strong value judgement underpinning the approach; in the other, the response is based exclusively on the practical recognition of the impossibility of the status quo.

In the past few years, the idea of degrowth has influenced a constellation of groups and networks operating at various levels. In many European countries it is not unusual to find 'clubs of degrowth' within larger social organizations, such as trade unions and political parties, usually but not exclusively sympathizing with the left. Many NGOs and associations have also contributed to the popularity of the concept and, if not explicitly, most of them adopt degrowth as the horizon of their action. These include organizations operating in fields as diverse as agroecology, environmental justice, defence of the territory, critical consumption, solidarity economy, eco-villages, alternative mobility (e.g. cycling) and urban gardens. Besides having forged partnerships with transition initiatives, permaculture associations and a wide range of environmental associations, the degrowth network has actively supported the causes of social movements such as the Association for the Taxation of Financial Transactions and for Citizens' Action (ATTAC) and rural campaigns in the global South such as Via Campesina. Since the eruption of the Great Recession, the movement has also espoused the social justice principles advanced by the Spanish *indignados* and the various global ramifications of the Occupy Wall Street network. In 2008, the representatives of various degrowth associations and a number of sympathetic intellectuals founded the Party for Degrowth (Parti Pour La Décroissance), which participated in the 2011 French cantonal elections.

In 2009, the scientific tenets of degrowth and its policy relevance were strengthened by the publication of a study commissioned by the UK Sustainable Development Commission. The report, which was then turned into a best-selling book titled *Prosperity without Growth: Economics for a Finite Planet*, built on over five years of work on lifestyles, values and the environment coordinated by the University of Surrey. It is a comprehensive analysis of the social and environmental imbalances generated by economic growth and a scathing critique of the political leadership's obsession with GDP, both in the stagnant economies of the global North and in the fast-growing emerging markets of the South. In its conclusions, the study echoes the critique and alternative agenda advanced by the followers of degrowth:

> Simplistic assumptions that capitalism's propensity for efficiency will stabilize the climate and solve the problem of resource scarcity are almost literally bankrupt. ... Our own relentless search for novelty and social status locks us into an iron cage of consumerism. ... There is an urgent need to fix the illiterate economics of relentless growth [and] we must transform the damaging social logic of consumerism. We've seen how a faulty economics drives and is driven by a distorted social logic. But we've also seen that a different economics is achievable. ... Neither ecological limits nor human nature constrain the possibilities here: only our capacity to believe in and work for change.[36]

Rethinking money

According to the New Economics Foundation (NEF), a think-tank closely cooperating with the transition and degrowth movements, the time has come for bold change. 'We must re-engineer our economies to tackle debt fuelled over-consumption, accelerating climatic instability and volatile energy prices underpinned by the approaching peak in global oil production', argues NEF in a report titled *The Great Transition*. 'It means re-thinking how we bank, generate energy, travel, and grow the food we depend on. It is a massive task that needs lots of organisations and people working together.'[37]

Food and energy production (or, rather, co-production) have been fundamental aspects of the new paradigm espoused by transition initiatives and degrowth movements across the world. In an effort to build sustainability and resilience, all these organizations and groups have advocated for various forms of economic re-localization. Besides redesigning production and consumption patterns, these movements have also contributed to a growing debate regarding the need to reinterpret the concept and goals of money. GDP is based on money. What is not monetized (or directly monetizable, as is the case with household services, voluntary work and self-production/self-consumption) does not get reflected in national income accounts, no matter how important it may be for economic progress and social well-being. Therefore, as the pillar on which the GDP development model is built, also the idea of money is being rethought. With a local flavour, of course.

In 2007, Hopkins and his colleagues at TTT launched the Totnes pound, a physical local currency backed by sterling and currently accepted in tens of businesses in the town. A local copy shop was contracted to print 10,000 Totnes pounds. Instead of being paid in sterling, they were happy to accept back 1,000 of the notes they had just run off.[38] The goal of the initiative was to ensure that wealth stayed in the community where it could be used in a more conscientious way with lower ecological impact and higher resilience. As described by the TTT folks, 'the Totnes

pound is based on a deep understanding of and critique of globalization, growth-based economics, the debt-based money system'.[39]
A local economy is like a 'leaky bucket': 'Our pensions, grants
and wages go into that bucket, but at the moment supermarkets,
chain stores and energy bills are drilling holes into it, leaving an
impoverished local economy.'[40] By contrast, local money 'helps
us think about our local economy, enquiring where our money
goes'.[41] And, if money is used for production and consumption
closer to home, 'we're going to pay more attention to how those
products are made, and the waste streams that result from them.'
Following Totnes's example, other transition initiatives have
introduced local currencies, also experimenting with new technologies. The Bristol and the Brixton 'pounds', for instance, allow
users to pay either with paper or with electronic currency via an
SMS.[42] Most associations affiliated to the degrowth movement,
too, have backed local or alternative currencies as a practical way
to promote autonomy from mainstream economic policies.

Local currencies (also known as complementary or community
currencies) are by no means a recent invention. Some of these
initiatives have been known for centuries and a number of experiments were already conducted during the Great Depression
in the 1930s. Yet, in the past few years they have multiplied
exponentially thanks to the supporting role of many civil society
groups, often in cooperation with sympathetic local authorities.
Local currencies are potentially very modern and, in their quin-
tessence, can be considered a reaction against top-down policies
of economic growth that are often imposed on local communities,
leaving the latter with little or no say over the way in which
common resources should be allocated and for what. These forms
of locally based money hold the promise of reducing capital flight,
shielding against global economic cycles, reining in the power of
commercial banks and supporting local economic activities. In a
word, they are seen as ways to democratize the economy.[43] Most

experiments are based on local exchange trading systems (LETS), one of the first forms of mutual credit, which allow members to earn credits by providing services or goods and spend them later by purchasing the same within the network of associates.

The alternative currency experiment SOL (solidarity-based electronic money), backed by the European Union's Equal initiative, and inaugurated in France in 2007, supports different types of ethical commerce. It is based on a broad partnership including two large mutual insurers, a cooperative bank, a leading cooperative company specializing in issuing vouchers, and three large regional governmental authorities (Île de France, Nord–Pas de Calais and Brittany). Currently, it is adopted in nine regions of the country and includes three different types of currency: (1) 'cooperation', which facilitates the circulation of money within the social economy; (2) 'commitment', which aims to make voluntary work visible and accountable, and is calculated in time; and (3) 'dedicated', which is a voucher given to specific target groups allowing them to buy basic goods or services. Given its focus on the social economy and voluntary work, SOL encourages users to invest money in those areas largely neglected by GDP accounts, including the non-profit sector. Importantly, SOL aims to reaffirm the role of money as a means rather than an end in itself so as to reconcile the economy with ethics, democracy and the environment.[44]

Most of these experiments have emerged out of barter markets and 'time banks', thereby constituting an evolution from the more traditional exchange of personal time in lieu of actual money. In most cases, new technologies have been an important contributing factor as most alternative currencies are in electronic format rather than on paper. Moreover, advances in information and communications systems have afforded new opportunities to citizens to organize horizontally and autonomously. For instance, Greece, a country heavily hit by the euro crisis, has experienced the introduction of alternative currencies as a means to regain democratic control over the economy. The virtual currency Ovolos (money in Ancient Greek) is an interesting example in so far as its promoters have explicitly developed new channels for bartering goods and services that may prove useful in the event of a sovereign default. Against the background of the country's economic situation and high unemployment rates, the project also aims to provide citizens that are usually excluded from conventional markets with an opportunity to benefit from economic and social exchange.

The Ovolos is conceived as a virtual currency – or 'social currency' as it is branded; the network of users currently consists of more than 5,000 members. Each member has an online account on the network's website and Ovolos units can be acquired through the sale or purchase of goods and services made available by the members themselves. This means that the larger the network of users, the more likely it is to find a variety of services and goods to exchange. The value of the Ovolos is safeguarded, because it is backed by the goods and services available within the network and it is possible to exchange it for euros at any time.[45] Ever since the economic crisis erupted in Greece, tens of local currencies have sprung up. Some of them have only a few hundred users and are mostly limited to small towns, but observers believe that the phenomenon is here to stay. According to George Stathakis, professor of political economy and vice chancellor of the University of Crete, 'there's been a boom in such networks all over Greece as there are so many huge gaps that have to be filled by new kinds of networks.'[46]

Alternative currencies also promote local production, thereby supporting regional development, reducing transport distances and, indirectly, alleviating ecological degradation and climate change. Germany has the highest number of alternative currencies in the world and Regiogeld is its largest network of institutionalized local money: it was established in 2003 and formally launched in 2006 through a registered umbrella association, the Regiogeld eV. Currently there are over seventy Regiogeld projects, of which the most famous is probably the Chiemgauer, initiated in a small Bavarian village in the Chiemgau region. The Regiogeld initiative spread quite quickly until 2008, after which various initiatives started diversifying operations, turning these local currencies into one of several instruments within an alternative regional cooperative network based on self-production. For example, the Bavarian Sterntaler is currently organized as a co-operative that includes small shops, a food-producing permaculture garden, a private LETS, a commercial barter system and a Regiogeld currency, as the overall medium of exchange. In 2012, the Chiemgauer too launched a microcredit initiative.[47]

The reasons why people have joined in vary. For some, local currencies are a way to improve sustainability at the local level and bring durable prosperity to the community. For some, these initiatives protect local economies against the speculative tendencies of financial markets. For others, an alternative form of currency is a valuable parachute should the eurozone eventually crash.[48] Although these currencies fall under a legal grey area and authorities are monitoring the situation, they are not illegal strictly speaking and governments treat them the same way as airlines' reward programmes. All associated businesses have signed formal contracts and are willing to bear a small loss (roughly 5 per cent) on every transaction, which then goes to local charities, kindergartens and other social initiatives. The Bundesbank – the most powerful central bank in Europe – estimated that in 2006 there were around $250,000 worth of local currencies circulating in at least sixteen regions of Germany. Currently, the estimated value is believed to be over $600,000.

According to one of the network's founders, 'participants in the alternative currencies movement want to change the money system.'[49] The German local currencies are indeed inspired by the work of monetary theorist, businessman and anarchist Silvio

Gesell, who first developed the idea of an interest-free currency after he witnessed the consequences of the 1890 depression in Argentina. Most Regiogeld currencies apply the principle of *demurrage*, which makes them depreciate over time, thereby creating an incentive for people to exchange them for services or goods rather than letting them sit in banks to earn interest. This way, money is given back the original role of 'means' rather than 'end', thus reducing the likelihood of financial speculation and encouraging investment in local enterprises.

Interest-free currencies also have the advantage of keeping the prices of goods and services relatively constant given that the regular circulation of a limited amount of money curbs inflation. Such a system provides a more fertile ground for a steady economy as it limits the risk of indebtedness. Conventional monetary systems, by contrast, rely on interest charged on money printed out of thin air, which basically founds the whole economic system on a vicious circle of debt. As argued by Regiogeld promoters, 'most people don't even know that by using money they are simply supporting a fundamentally undemocratic system of consumption and over-consumption known as the "debt trap".'[50] They hope that, with the proliferation of alternative currencies through the main European economy, there may be room for an open and democratic debate throughout the European Union as to what money is really for. Echoing the fans of degrowth, they believe that the time has come for people to have a say over the ultimate values and goals of macroeconomic policy. In order to do so, people must be given the power to rule money, rather than being ruled by it.

The sandwich model

According to world-renowned environmentalist Paul Hawken, change is driven by a silent multitude that, largely ignored by politicians and the media, is putting human society back on a sustainability track with respect to its living environment and ecosystems. In his opinion, transition initiatives and degrowth associations are just a few examples of a much larger social movement, the largest in history: 'just like nature, it is organizing from the bottom up, in every city, town, and culture'.[51] While recognizing the lack of a unifying ideology or charismatic leader, Hawken is convinced that this movement is nevertheless animated by the same principles and carries forward the best of mankind, 'a living intelligence that creates miracles every second'.

Although this may be an overly optimistic assessment, there is little doubt that some of these organizations have been leading the way in the reconfiguration of the dominant economic model and the 'iron cage' represented by GDP growth. By experimenting with alternative methods of co-production and new patterns of consumption, some of these groups are evolving 'a lifestyle designed for permanence', to paraphrase E.F. Schumacher, the forefather of contemporary environmentalism.[52]

At the same time, just like most civil-society-led activities, these experiences are still grappling with issues of scale as they struggle to stimulate change at the macro-level. While transition initiatives have been very successful at kick-starting a 'practical' revolution in some countries, especially in small municipalities in Europe, their reluctance to get involved in more advocacy work may eventually limit their capacity to promote macroeconomic reforms. Moreover, as they grow in terms of numbers and resources, some of their projects might end up turning into conventional economic ventures, similar to the experience of the co-operative movement in the 1900s. The degrowth network has yet to achieve a global critical mass, let alone elicit a substantial political appeal. When it launched its political manifesto and participated in (local) elections, as it did in France in 2011, it failed get any of its candidates elected.

Similarly, not all alternative currencies aim to rethink the money system. Some of them are mere survival strategies in times of economic recession. As already happened in the past, it is possible that some of these local currencies will disappear once countries (and their communities) return to business-as-usual economy. Moreover, the risk of moral hazard does not spare alternative money either. For instance, the Liberty dollar, a private currency produced in the US with a circulation of over 250,000 users, ceased to exist in 2011 due to fraud and counterfeit. So, while local currencies experience a boom at present (especially in crisis-ridden Europe), their future role and expansion capacity remains uncertain.

Undoubtedly, the most important contribution of all these initiatives has been practical: they have challenged preconceived notions and conventional wisdom by showing that alternative ways of life are not just possible but also desirable. Ideas and theories do not travel on their own. They need legs to walk on. And grassroots movements provide the most fertile ground for 'trickle-up' processes, whereby change is first achieved locally and then transferred to the top.

This is what Lester Brown, the president of the Earth Policy Institute in Washington, calls the 'sandwich model'. This ideal situation for rapid and historic progress generally occurs 'when mounting grassroots pressure for change merges with a national leadership committed to the same change'.[53] Many social reforms are possible when societies reach tipping points or cross key thresholds. Once that happens, change may come rapidly and often unpredictably.

As the Argentinian example demonstrates, crises can open up new windows of opportunity. They allow citizens and policymakers (or at least those who have the cognitive capacity and indispensable curiosity) to see through the veil of complacency erected by conventional thinking. It is then the task of these individuals to build the necessary popular support to trigger meaningful change. Our societies have reached an unprecedented tipping point, whereby not just an economic crisis but a convergence of crises, from climate change to social unrest, are ravaging the world. This may well be the moment that many progressive intellectuals and civil society activists have been waiting for.

Supremacy and resistance

Anyone who believes exponential growth can go on forever in a finite world is either a madman or an economist.

Kenneth Ewart Boulding

A small truth is better than a great lie.

Leonardo da Vinci

In a paper presented at the forum on Environmental Quality in a Growing Economy in 1966, the US economist Kenneth Boulding compared the GDP economy to a cowboy, a symbol of 'the illimitable plains' generally associated 'with reckless, exploitative, romantic, and violent behavior'.[1] In the cowboy economy, production and consumption are regarded as supreme values. The success of the economy is measured by the amount of throughput, a part of which 'is extracted from the reservoirs of raw materials and noneconomic objects' while another part 'is output into the reservoirs of pollution'. By contrast, he argued, what we would need is a 'spaceman' economy, in which the earth has become 'a single spaceship, without unlimited reservoirs of anything, either for extraction or for pollution'. In this scenario, human beings will need to find their place 'in a cyclical ecological system which is capable of continuous reproduction of material form'. In the spaceman economy, throughput is by no means a desideratum, and should be regarded as 'something to be minimized rather than maximized'. The essential measure of success for the economy will not be the degree of production and consumption, but the nature, extent, quality and complexity of all human and natural resources: 'In the spaceman economy, what we are primarily concerned with is stock maintenance, and any technological change which results in the maintenance of a given total stock with a lessened throughput (that is, less production and consumption) is clearly a gain.'

In 2012, Harvard economist Kenneth Rogoff, formerly chief economist at the IMF and recipient of the 2011 Deutsche Bank Prize in Financial Economics, penned an editorial titled 'Rethinking the Growth Imperative', in which he lamented that modern macroeconomics has long treated rapid and continuous GDP growth as the 'be-all and end-all of policy'.[2] Reflecting on the root causes of the current financial and economic crisis, he concluded that 'there is a certain absurdity to the obsession with maximizing long-term average income growth in perpetuity, to the neglect of other risks and considerations.'

Although the number of GDP 'sceptics' seems to have grown in recent times, the majority of opinion leaders and influential economists are still praising the wonders of economic growth. Funnily enough, some of those who criticize GDP today were among its most devoted worshippers only a few years ago. Social psychologists would probably explain the historical success of GDP in terms of 'groupthink', a term which refers to the faulty decisions taken by groups when undue pressure ultimately leads to the deterioration of mental efficiency, reality testing and moral judgement.[3] Indeed, collective dynamics, especially within closed circles, can easily trigger self-censorship, as people may be afraid of deviating from what is considered the general consensus. In turn, this strengthens conventional wisdom and contributes to reinforcing credence in accepted norms, in spite of their logical invalidity. Nowhere is this phenomenon as common as with the so-called experts, who strive to defend their intellectual 'rank' and feel like no one else the pressure of peers. This constant need for recognition often limits their capacity to raise doubts and present alternative possibilities, lest they may be derided and marginalized by colleagues. Among the symptoms of groupthink one finds the illusion of invulnerability and unanimity, the belief in the inherent morality of the group, the stereotyped views of out-groups and the ridicule of dissenters.[4] As remarked by historian Tony Judt, society ends up paying a huge price because of such complacency. Indeed, a close circle of opinion or ideas, into which discontent or opposition is never allowed, 'loses its capacity to respond energetically or imaginatively to new challenges'.[5]

On a visit to the London School of Economics in 2009, the Queen asked why no economist had predicted the 2008 financial crisis. As a matter of fact, there were economists, civil society activists and public intellectuals who had warned against the growing indebtedness and instability of the financial system long before the fall of Lehman Brothers. Even some film documentaries had focused on the risk of an imminent crisis as early as 2006.[6] Yet the discipline and its masters had refused to listen. In response, the Queen got a letter undersigned by a group of renowned economists. The letter conceded that the discipline was driven by a 'psychology of denial' gripping the analytical capacity of academic economists amid a 'wishful thinking combined with hubris' permeating the financial world. And it concluded: 'your Majesty, the failure to foresee the timing, extent and severity of the crisis and to head it off, while it had many causes, was principally a failure of the collective imagination of many bright people, both in this country and internationally, to understand the risks to the system as a whole.'[7]

Nobel laureate Paul Krugman, too, recognized the groupthink dynamic governing economic circles. In a long editorial for the *New York Times Magazine*, he admitted that there were a few economists who challenged the assumption of rational behaviour, questioned the belief that financial markets can be trusted and pointed to the long history of financial crises that had devastating economic consequences: 'But they were swimming against the tide, unable to make much headway against a pervasive and, in retrospect, foolish complacency.'[8] Groupthink is steered by charismatic leaders and recognized authorities in the field, who act as 'mindguards'.[9] These are individuals who act as informational filters, providing limited information to the group and, consciously or subconsciously, utilizing a variety of more or less subtle strategies to control dissent and direct the decision-making process towards a specific, limited range of possibilities. The result is unconditional acceptance of views that may be dead wrong, in spite (or rather, because) of the illustrious pedigree of those who take them. Influenced by this herd mentality, experts deliberately choose to ignore critical or warning voices. Often they do so to reinforce their own status and protect their discipline. In sum, they seek to strengthen their grip on power, and more often than not they succeed. Just look at the key players in the Obama administration tasked with addressing the economic crisis. The very same 'experts' that led the culture of denial and profited from it for decades are in power. Again.

There is no doubt that the invention of GDP has given economics a primary role in society and politics. Conformity among mainstream economists has been pervasive, in spite of the few critical voices presented in this book. And this strategic unanimity has helped strengthen their discipline vis-à-vis other social sciences. Complaining about the lack of consensus on principles and measures of progress in political and social analysis, a colleague of mine once told me: 'At least economists all agree on

GDP maximisation as the ultimate goal of economic development. What do other social scientists agree on?'

In 1941, Kuznets admitted that the measurement of national income should not be regarded as a morally neutral process, because it is continually 'affected by implicit or explicit value judgments'. Looking at the enthusiasm with which his creation was being welcomed by economists and statisticians, he observed that

> the apparent relative unanimity produced by empirical writings on national income is due largely to the estimators' unconscious acceptance of one social philosophy and their natural reluctance to face such fundamental issues as would reveal that estimates are conditioned by controversial criteria.[10]

Yet, in a world desperately seeking uncontested truths, the development of national income statistics transformed economics from a philosophical reflection on human societies (often based on anecdotal evidence and approximated estimates) into a 'hard' science, supposedly characterized by immutable laws and perfect models. If William Petty's calculations in the late 1600s aimed at turning political economy into a perfect science like mathematics, the systematic adoption of GDP as the standard measure of economic progress went way beyond that: it made economics the most powerful of all disciplines. Economists reclaimed their independent epistemological status and new faculties were created amid a growing and unprecedented popularity in society at large. Students flocked to business schools, as this came to be conventionally regarded as the best way to get an 'important' and awesomely remunerated job.

Ever since, economists have become opinion leaders, government advisers and sought-after consultants. Every quarter, when GDP estimates and projections are officially released by statistical agencies, herds of alleged economic 'experts' pop up everywhere in the media, populating news bulletins and talk shows. They tell us that sustained economic growth is essential to job creation and present innumerable recipes to strengthen economic performance. If GDP goes up, they cheer. If it goes down, they mourn and blame political leaders for doing too little to prop up the economy.

Conflicts of interest have prospered in the GDP era. Many academic economists have left their desks to be flown to Washington, London and Frankfurt. Or, more recently, they have relocated to Beijing and Singapore. They are regularly appointed board members of public enterprises, private corporations and so-called public benefit foundations. Governments hire them to advise on macroeconomic policies and growth strategies. Multinational corporations pay them handsome consultancy fees to sharpen their competitive advantage and increase their market shares. They have filled the ranks of international institutions, from the IMF and the World Bank down to the myriad local institutions dedicated to support development in poor countries. In a word, they have been successful at building the most powerful paradigm of all times: that GDP growth is the panacea; that massive production and consumption equate development; and that this is all countries need to strive for.

According to degrowth ideologue Serge Latouche, the new heroes of the day are mostly 'the products of business schools, which might be more accurately described as "schools of economic warfare"'.

> These strategists are intent on doing all they can to outsource costs, which are borne by their employees, their subcontracts, the countries of the South, their clients, states and public services, future generations and, above all, nature, which has become both a supplier of resources and a dustbin.[11]

The American statistician W.E. Deming is generally (though, perhaps, incorrectly) reported as having said that to measure is tantamount to manage. This is true in many fields, as the proliferation of data has made decision-making fundamentally dependent on those who produce numbers. But GDP is not just a number. It is *the* number par excellence. This is why, in the case of GDP statistics, to measure is *to rule*. Quite aptly, the English language supports this intimate connection between measurements and power. A 'ruler' can indeed be either a head of government (a monarch, dictator or a democratically elected president) or a measuring device, an apparently harmless straight-edged strip used for drawing lines and measuring lengths.

The invention of GDP did not only mark the era in which economics (and economists) became an all-powerful force in society. It also ushered in a new age of market supremacy. As economic growth became the most important goal of politics, the 'producers' of growth felt their reign of uncontested leadership had finally arrived. Through national income statistics, each industry could boast of its contribution to the wealth of the nation and reclaim its share of public recognition for that. Moreover, as GDP masked the negative externalities of industrial production, all industries (especially the heavy polluters) ended up getting a facelift, a kind of cosmetic purification. Thanks to this statistical laundromat, their 'bads' magically disappeared, as society could only see the money being 'generated'.

GDP has also brought about a fundamental redesign of employment policies, a traditional preoccupation of all policymakers interested in staying in office. As it came to be conventionally assumed that economic growth meant more employment opportunities, politicians have surrendered to the magical power of business. 'Pump money into the economy and growth will generate jobs' has become an adage among government leaders throughout the world. The conceptual boundaries between developmental states, where central governments steer macroeconomic planning, and free markets, where business takes the lead and governments' action is generally limited to some form of regulation, have become more and more blurred. On the one hand, as a strong business sector is essential to sustain economic growth, centralistic political elites have been forced to devolve power and competencies to corporations, even though governments may in turn control the latter through some type of formal or de facto arrangement. On the other hand, the objective of reaching ever-higher growth targets has given business an opportunity to demand stronger public investment in the economy, which has resulted in massive government spending programmes and huge volumes of subsidies for corporations also in allegedly free-market societies. The principle is simple: if GDP growth is what society wants and business is instrumental in achieving it, then the latter should be rewarded for this all-important social role.

Trade unions, too, have fallen into the GDP trap. In order to preserve jobs, they have made historic concessions to both business and government. In the West, this has meant further deregulation and less stringent laws for corporations. In the East, it has resulted in a blank cheque for state-controlled industries. In many instances, unabated devotion to GDP-led employment policies has turned trade unions into 'socially conservative' agents, separating them from more progressive groups within civil society. A wedge has been driven in, especially in relation to the ecological movement, in so far as stricter environmental regulations to slow down or halt growth in some industrial sectors have been interpreted by unions as a threat to the labour force.

Needless to say, corporations have fed this type of distrust across sectors while doing all they can to capitalize on the advantages presented by a globalized labour market. Almost invariably they have adopted the threat of relocation to countries with laxer regulations with a view to opposing stricter environmental rules and reining in workers' associations. Perhaps surreptitiously, they have institutionalized corporate blackmail in their management strategies, a reality that has been largely internalized by society too. As a consequence, most trade unions, as well as millions of workers, have become defenders of GDP growth at all costs. As Yale emeritus professor Charles Lindblom wrote in 1982, economic growth has turned markets into 'prisons'. Whatever attempt at rethinking the growth imperative by limiting the dominance of business is 'followed immediately – swiftly – by the punishment of unemployment'. This form of punishment, argued Lindblom, is not simply reactive. It is a proactive interference with policymaking, a type of 'prospective punishment': the mere suggestion that some type of change may occur is immediately attacked with 'an automatic punishing recoil'.[12]

GDP is not just a statistical metric. It represents a way of or-ganizing society. Rather than a neutral number, it is a powerful political tool. Its origin and development were deeply intertwined with the most fundamental political struggles of the past century. It was initially employed as 'war machine' in the Second World War, allowing the US to assess the projected capacity of its economy and wage the war on two fronts without curtailing internal consump-tion. It was then used as a propaganda device during the bipolar rivalry between capitalism and the Soviet empire. At that time, achieving sustained rates of economic growth meant more than simply scaling up industrial production: it was propagandized as building a better way of life. On the one hand, the Soviet Union rejected the GDP metric and adopted a different model of economic account, largely derived from Marxist economic theory. It also challenged Western countries through ambitious policies to stimulate economic growth and allegedly achieve the world's highest development standards. On the other hand, the US discredited Soviet statistics and went all out to demonstrate that political manipulation was behind the purported economic miracle of the USSR. These differences in statistical accounting triggered a proxy war involving secret services and economic experts, which only ended with the fall of the Soviet Union, when GDP finally triumphed and became the only international standard for the measurement of economic performance.

The history of GDP was that of the quest for power that continues to affect our political life today. In his influential 1989 book *The Rise and Fall of the Great Powers*, Harvard historian Paul Kennedy concluded that a country's wealth and productive power (at least in so far as it relates to that of its contemporaries) is one of the essential determinants of its global status.[13] Looking at how global governance has been shaped in the past decades, one could not agree more. The world has been dominated by a hierarchy of countries, carefully selected on the basis of their GDP credentials, traditionally led by the US. Those who fall from grace, such as stagnant European economies, are increasingly treated as pariahs. Those who do not perform extraordinarily, such as most of the so-called 'developing' world, will never be invited to the ball. Currently, all eyes are on the so-called emerging powers. Why? Because they have rocked global economy with their stunning GDP growth rates. Never mind, of course, the cost in terms of ecological degradation and social impoverishment that the achievement of this status has implied. To paraphrase Boulding, the world is still run by cowboys, plains appear endless, and the gold fever fuels human greed.

Yet things may be about to change. The outburst of the Great Recession has had a double, albeit potentially contradictory, effect. On the one hand, it has awakened some progressive world leaders and opinion-makers with regard to the 'dark side' of GDP. This has triggered the frantic work of a number of commissions and the publication of studies and reports on the measurement of economic performance and social well-being, some of which actually pre-date the 2008 financial collapse. On the other hand, widespread unemployment and social discontent have rearmed conservative forces, which see GDP growth as the only escape from the current economic downturn. In their opinion, these are not times to challenge the GDP paradigm as what the world needs is more growth and quickly. For these advocates of consumption, governments must find a way (possibly, any way) to get people back onto their shopping sprees. It is because of these calls for more productivity that several governments in battered European economies have been toying with the idea of eliminating public holidays.

In some cases, institutions have tried to combine both views, but results have been disappointing. The European Union's 2020 strategy, for instance, speaks proudly of 'smart, sustainable and inclusive growth'.[14] Yet, despite the commitment to building a low-carbon economy (whose targets remain largely unmet by many member states), most of these widely heralded goals are the outcome of political expediency rather than a serious reconsideration of conventional wisdom. They usually call for the incorporation of vaguely defined indicators of well-being into macroeconomic planning, but still rely predominantly on GDP as the cornerstone of policies. Moreover, they resort to the debatable argument of decoupling growth from its negative externalities, by arguing that, with a polished GDP, economic development can be attained without causing imbalances and injustices.

It is difficult to make predictions with regard to which of these two contrasting views will eventually prevail. There continues to be some interest in revising GDP statistics, but as the crisis worsens (especially in the US and Europe) the risk is that the topic will lose relevance for public opinion. While the world's attention is increasingly concentrated on credit ratings and yield spreads of sovereign debt obligations, it appears as if whatever change may occur will be cosmetic at best. In the UK, for instance, the fanfare surrounding the government's plan to measure well-being has resulted in four generic 'how do you feel' questions being surveyed by national statisticians. The high-level commission launched by the French president in 2008 has provided an important reference point for many experts, but it has not (yet) resulted in tangible reforms and the website has not been updated since the publication of the report in 2009. Moreover, in the 2012 presidential elections the debate revolved exclusively around GDP growth, with no reference to alternative approaches.

What most of these technical attempts fail to see is the profound political nature of GDP. Either out of naivety or political correctness, they do not recognize that behind an apparent mathematical neutrality lies a world of power struggles and conflicts of interest that should be identified and disentangled if real change is to be achieved. In its popularized usage, GDP has become a social construct and a hegemonic political discourse. Over time, it has endured many challenges. In the past few decades, tons of papers have been written and a myriad alternative indicators have been produced. Yet none of them, thus far, has been able to dethrone this magical number.

GDP is built on a great lie. This lie says that markets are the only producers of wealth. What is not priced, what does not involve a formal financial transaction based on money, does not count – no matter how important it may be for our social and economic well-being. Price tags are the ultimate symbol of GDP. Continuous production and endless consumption are its underlying values. Durability, reusability and self-production are its worst enemies. Things that last are detrimental to GDP, because they only get priced (and thus counted) once. Things that we produce for ourselves are even worse, because they are not priced at all. In this paradigm, households are reduced to cages of consumers. If families do not own two or three television sets, at least a couple of cars, innumerable kitchen appliances and a universe of utensils that must be continuously replaced, then they are publicly scorned. If they are not obsessed with shopping, they are considered a threat to national security.

Nature, the ultimate provider of all richness, is enslaved and devalued. GDP gives mankind the illusion that growth is about production, when it actually should be viewed as a transfer. Mankind does not produce anything. It simply turns natural wealth into money. And puts it up for sale, in what looks like the most vicious system of prostitution, the most disastrous Ponzi scheme of history.[15] According to E.F. Schumacher, the GDP paradigm 'consumes the very basis on which it has been erected' and 'lives on irreplaceable capital which it cheerfully treats as income'.[16] The process through which this illusion is created can be compared to the securitization of the subprime mortgages that led to the 2008 financial disaster. Just as in that case, we are getting a loan (from nature) that we are not going to be able to repay. In the meantime, we slice it up into an endless sequence of small loans (that we call production), which we then sell on to the market in return for money (we call this process consumption). These micro-loans are then packaged by our governments and sold back to everybody, in terms of pollution and environmental degradation. Often it is the poor countries that pick up most of our debt with nature, especially when they face droughts, floods and other types of climate-change-related disasters. But future generations will definitely be the payers of last resort. They will be charged all-time high interests, which essentially cannot be repaid. It is estimated that it took Great Britain around sixty years to double its economy when the Industrial Revolution began. Then it took the US around fifty years to double its economy at the beginning of the twentieth century. Several East and Southeast Asian countries today have been doubling their economies every ten years.[17] While a few decades ago the concept of 'future genera-tions' was felt with some distance, nowadays we are becoming increasingly aware that – at this rate of growth – the future is quickly catching up with us. Which means that the generation to face nature's debt collectors may very well be our children's.

Although the media are hung up on the financial and social consequences of the Great Recession, our present economic turmoil is just the tip of the iceberg of a more profound and widespread systemic crisis caused by the dogma of infinite GDP growth. Energy resources are irremediably running out. Countries compete to get access to the few untapped oil fields in what looks like an unprecedented global scramble for fuel. As climate change melts ice caps, governments and oil companies jump at the insane but ludicrous deal of offshore drilling in the Arctic. Meanwhile, nations endowed with precious minerals have been ravaged by wars, coups, corruption and terrorism. For these countries, a resource-rich subsoil has become the ultimate curse, as extractive industries have been willing to do whatever it takes to secure profits at the expense of local communities. Paradoxically, most societies endowed with a wealth of natural capital have become the poorest in the GDP world.

By definition, infinite growth on a planet of finite resources is incompatible with global justice, at least in so far as it triggers a dangerous zero-sum game. As Mahatma Gandhi once said, the earth provides enough to satisfy 'every man's need', but not 'every man's greed'. Climate change has eventually made this simple (but largely rejected) truth self-evident. As our planet can no longer absorb increasing quantities of greenhouse gases, economic growth in our part of the globe becomes incompatible with an equal amount of growth elsewhere. The global village has become a global dustbin. After sweeping the trash under the carpet for years, there is no space left. When we try to shovel more garbage from this side, it inevitably comes out on the other side. By reasserting the need for growth in the most industrialized societies, we are condemning economically less advanced societies to perpetual poverty.

At the political level, the GDP dogma has also impoverished democracy. It has glorified the role of technocrats, thus turning politics into a matter for experts. It has perpetuated a culture of violence, exemplified by increasing military expenses. It also has cleaned up the reputation of polluting industries, which have been lauded for their contribution to the national income instead of being punished for undermining collective welfare. At the global level, it has contributed to reducing the space for participation, thus reinforcing a system in which only an elite of big powers can control energy resources while pulling the strings of global governance.

GDP has also exerted a profound impact on our societies. It has reduced the time spent on leisure and amplified the burden of work. Technological innovation has not necessarily meant a better quality of life. By contrast, it has often brought an additional layer of complexity. Although nowadays workers achieve more with an hour of their time than they used to in the past, their targets have shifted accordingly. With more technology to help them, they are indeed expected to sustain higher production rates. This has generated a vicious circle of increasing pressure and continuous burnout. Our work–life balance, too, has been irremediably affected. Ever more demanding careers make it hard for women and men to have children. Children often spend more time watching television or playing video games than they do with their busy parents. Spare time is also encapsulated into pre-packaged forms of entertainment. As free-of-charge public spaces have retreated, a flood of costly opportunities has inundated our lives. Shopping malls have replaced public squares as places where people meet. Affluent societies are awash with sports centres, gyms, pools and various other forms of private club. Nowadays, it has become virtually impossible to do any outdoor activity without a spate of 'indispensable' gadgets (e.g. glossy uniforms, shirts, caps, gloves, sunglasses, etc.) made available at gigantic megastores. Even jogging, arguably the simplest and lightest form of physical activity, has become a resource-intensive experience, while marathons have systematically turned into a phenomenon of collective hysteria, where thousands of people litter their cities with plastic bags, empty bottles, flyers and other types of trash.

GDP was designed as a war device. That war did not end in 1945, but has continued ever since. It turned into an endless war against social equilibria, natural environments and non-renewable resources, in which consumers became the new foot soldiers; ultimately, a war against our own future on this planet. To paraphrase Lindblom, one may say that GDP has not only 'imprisoned our thinking about politics and economics',[18] but has also held captive our capacity to reinvent our social environment. However, 'where there are prisons, there are also jailbreaks.'[19] In this process of emancipation, statistical reforms are important but grossly insufficient. A credible challenge to the GDP paradigm can only come from an open debate in society involving civil society groups, political parties, the media, sectoral organizations, religious groups, as well as everybody else. Ideally, this process should involve citizens not only in the most industrialized countries but also in less affluent nations, particularly in the new emerging powers, which are nowadays the beacons of global economic growth. Not just the metrics, but also the underlying politics of GDP must be fundamentally challenged. For starters, this would require rethinking the principles and goals of economics as a human discipline and, quite importantly, the role of economists in society. But, more significantly, it would imply a fundamental reappropriation of our political space. By challenging GDP, we stand a chance to regain control over our political, social and economic institutions. By reasserting the creativity of life over the fallacy of growth, we fight for the survival of humankind. This is the most important struggle of all time.

Notes

INTRODUCTION

1. IPCC, *Emissions Scenarios* (Cambridge: Cambridge University Press, 2000).
2. See *The Economist Debates* at www.economist.com/debate/days/view/503#mod_module
3. In 2007, this was the opening sentence of the OECD's website. See also OECD, *Statistics, Policy and Knowledge 2007: Measuring and Fostering the Progress of Societies* (Paris: OECD, 2008). The quotation is taken from the back cover of the volume.
4. A. Smith, *The Wealth of Nations* (London: Methuen 1904 [1776]), book II, ch. III, sect. II.3.1.
5. Ibid. II.3.4.
6. K. Marx, *Capital: A Critique of Political Economy*, Vol. II: *The Process of Circulation of Capital* (Chicago: C.H. Kerr, 1909 [1885]), III.XIX.39.
7. S. Kuznets, (1934) 'National Income, 1929–1932', report presented to the 73rd US Congress, 2d session, Senate document no. 124, p. 7. Reprinted as 'National Income, 1929–1932, *NBER Bulletin* 49, 7 June 1934, p. 1.
8. S. Kuznets, *National Income and Capital Formation, 1919–1935* (New York: National Bureau of Economic Research, 1937), p. 4.
9. See Bureau of Economic Analysis, *Measuring the Economy: A Primer on GDP and the National Income and Product Accounts* (Washington DC: Department of Commerce, 2007).

10. Two other critical indicators are the gross national income (GNI) and the gross domestic income (GDI). The GNI is GDP less net taxes on production and imports, less wages and rents paid to employees and firms residing abroad, but plus the wages and items received from the rest of the world. The GDI measures the purchasing power of the total incomes generated by domestic production. It is often used by government and central banks to gauge economic activity based on income and corresponds to GDP when calculated through the income approach.

11. T. Foertsch, 'A Victory for Taxpayers and the Economy', *Heritage Foundation*, 2006, WebMemo#1082.

12. Speech given by G.W. Bush to employees at O'Hare Airport, Chicago, on 27 September 2001, http://georgewbush-whitehouse.archives.gov/news/releases/2001/09/20010927-1.html (accessed 15 July 2012); 'Britain needs you to Shop, says Blair', *Telegraph*, 28 September 2001.

13. 'Shopping is Patriotic, Leaders Say', *National Post*, 28 September 2001.

14. 'America's New War: Giuliani on Local Radio Show', 21 September 2001, transcripts provided by CNN.com at http://transcripts.cnn.com/transcripts/0109/21/se.20.html (accessed 15 July 2012).

15. 'Shopping is Patriotic, Leaders Say'.

16. F. Schneider and D. Enste, 'Hiding in the Shadows: The Growth of the Underground Economy', *Economic Issues* 30 (Brussels: International Monetary Fund, 2002).

17. All these authors are cited in A.O. Hirschman, 'Rival Interpretations of the Market Society', *Journal of Economic Literature* 20 (December 1982), pp. 1464–5.

18. A. Toynbee, *Lectures on the Industrial Revolution of the Eighteenth Century in England* (London: Rivingstons, 1884), p. 84.

19. T. Carlyle, 'The Present Time', *Latter Day Pamphlets*, Issue 1, February 1850.

20. European Commission, *GDP and Beyond: Measuring Progress in a Changing World*, 2009, COM/2009/0433 final.

21. J.E. Stiglitz, A. Sen and J.-P. Fitoussi, *Report by the Commission on the Measurement of Economic Performance and Progress*, 2009, www.stiglitz-se-fitoussi.fr, p. 13.

CHAPTER 1

1. N. Canny, *From Reformation to Resistance: Ireland, 1534–1660* (Dublin: Helicon, 1987).

2. A. Roncaglia, *Petty: The Origins of Political Economy* (Armonk, NY:

M.E. Sharpe, 1985), p. 5.

3. M. Poovey, *A History of the Modern Fact* (Chicago and London: University of Chicago Press, 1998).

4. Ibid., p. 124.

5. W. Petty, *The Economic Writings of Sir William Petty* (Fairfield, NJ: Augustus M. Kelley, 1986), p. 53.

6. Poovey, *A History of the Modern Fact*, p. 127.

7. Ibid., p. 127.

8. Petty, *The Economic Writings of Sir William Petty*, p. 454.

9. Ibid., p. 267.

10. Poovey, *A History of the Modern Fact*.

11. Roncaglia, *Petty*.

12. V. Kapuria-Foreman and M. Perlman, 'An Economic Historian's Economist: Remembering Simon Kuznets', *Economic Journal* 105 (433) (1995): 1524–47.

13. Quoted in US Department of Commerce, 'GDP: One of the Great Inventions of the 20th Century', *Survey of Current Business*, January 2000, p. 6.

14. C.S. Carson, 'The History of the United States National Income and Product Accounts: The Development of an Analytical Tool', *Review of Income and Wealth*, 21(2) (1975): 153–81.

15. Ibid.

16. Kapuria-Foreman and Perlman, 'An Economic Historian's Economist', p. 1530.

17. Ibid., p. 1531; Carson 'The History of the United States National Income and Product Accounts'.

18. C.S. Carson, 'The Conference on Research in Income and Wealth: The Early Years', in Ernst R. Berndt and Jack E. Triplett (eds), *Fifty Years of Economic Measurement: The Jubilee of the Conference on Research in Income and Wealth* (Chicago: University of Chicago Press, 1991).

19. S. Kuznets, *National Income and Capital Formation, 1919–1935* (New York: National Bureau of Economic Research, 1937), p. 4.

20. NBER, *Studies in Income and Wealth*, Vol. III (New York: National Bureau of Economic Research, 1939).

21. The quotation is from Carson, 'The Conference on Research in Income and Wealth', p. 6.

22. Ibid., p. 7.

23. Carson, 'The History of the United States National Income and Product Accounts'.

24. Kapuria-Foreman and Perlman, 'An Economic Historian's Economist'. See also R. Nathan, 'GNP and Military Mobilization', *Journal*

of Evolutionary Economics 4(1) (1994): 1–16.

25. J. Lacey, *Keep from All Thoughtful Men: How US Economists Won World War Two* (Annapolis, MD: Naval Institute Press, 2011).

26. Carson, 'The History of the United States National Income and Product Accounts'.

27. Lacey, *Keep from All Thoughtful Men*, p. 88.

28. Quoted in ibid., p. 104.

29. E. Lundberg, 'Simon Kuznets' Contribution to Economics', *Swedish Journal of Economics* 73(4) (1971): 444–59. See also Carson 'The History of the United States National Income and Product Accounts'.

30. Quoted in US Department of Commerce, 'GDP', p. 8.

31. C. Cobb, T. Halstead and K. Rowe, 'If the GDP is Up, Why is America Down?', *Atlantic Monthly*, October 1995, p. 6.

32. J. Rowe, (2008) 'Our Phony Economy', *Harper's*, June 2008.

33. J.K. Galbraith, 'The National Accounts: Arrival and Impact', in N. Cousins (ed.), *Reflections of America: Commemorating the Statistical Abstract Centennial* (Washington, DC: US Department of Commerce, Bureau of the Census, 1980), p. 80.

34. See 'Preface' to NBER, *Studies in Income and Wealth* (New York: National Bureau of Economic Research, 1946).

35. S. Kuznets, 'Government Product and National Income', in E. Lundberg (ed.), *Income and Wealth* (Cambridge: Cambridge University Press, 1951), pp. 184–5.

36. R. Higgs, 'Wartime Prosperity? A Reassessment of the US Economy in the 1940s', *Journal of Economic History* 52(1) (1992): 41–60.

37. Kapuria-Foreman and Perlman, 'An Economic Historian's Economist: Remembering Simon Kuznets'.

38. T.A. Khomenko, 'Estimation of Gross Social Product and Net Material Product in the USSR', Discussion Paper Series no. 172, Institute for Economic Research, Hitotsubashi University, Tokyo, July 2006.

39. E.P. Gorbunov, 'The Gross Social Product' (1970), in A.M. Prokhorov (ed.), *Great Soviet Encyclopaedia* (New York: Macmillan/ London: Collier Macmillan, 1974–83).

40. P. Studenski, 'Methods of Estimating National Income in Russia', in NBER, *Studies in Income and Wealth*, p. 199.

41. Khomenko, 'Estimation of Gross Social Product and Net Material Product in the USSR'.

42. Studenski, 'Methods of Estimating National Income in Russia'.

43. See Gorbunov, 'The Gross Social Product'.

44. Ibid.

45. According to scholars of the Soviet economy, the mere distinction between a physical good and a service was not 'economically

significant'. The only important difference was 'between production organized under the prevailing rules of the society and flowing
through its channels and that not so organized and carried on'. The
former was a part of national production and national income, while
the latter was not. See Studenski, 'Methods of Estimating National
Income in Russia', p. 200.

46. J.H. Noren, 'CIA's Analysis of the Soviet Economy', in G.K. Haines
    and R.E. Leggett (eds), *Watching the Bear: Essays on CIA's Analysis
    of the Soviet Union* (Washington, DC: Central Intelligence Agency,
    2003).

47. Ibid.

48. Cited in ibid.

49. Ibid.

50. B. Kostinsky and M. Belkindas, 'Official Soviet Gross National Prod-
    uct Accounting', in *Measuring Soviet GNP: Problems and Solutions*,
    report from the conference sponsored by the CIA's Office of Soviet
    Analysis, 1990, pp. 183–92.

51. See Khrushchev's 'Theses on the Seven-Year Soviet Economic
    Plan, 1959–65', mentioned by Noren, 'CIA's Analysis of the Soviet
    Economy'.

52. Noren, 'CIA's Analysis of the Soviet Economy'.

53. M. Boretsky, 'The Tenability of the CIA's Estimates of Soviet
    Economic Growth', *Journal of Comparative Economics* 11 (1987):
    517–42.

54. V. Treml, 'Perestroika and Soviet Statistics', in *The Impact of Gor-
    bachev's Policies on Soviet Economic Statistics*, report from the con-
    ference sponsored by the CIA's Office of Soviet Analysis, 1988, pp.
    51–68. See also F. Kushnirsky, (1988) 'New Challenges to Soviet Of-
    ficial Statistics: A Methodological Survey', in ibid., pp. 11–26.

55. R.E. Ericson, 'The Soviet Statistical Debate: Khanin vs. TsSU',
    paper presented at Hoover–Rand conference, Stanford University,
    March 1988.

56. Kostinsky and Belkindas, 'Official Soviet Gross National Product
    Accounting'.

57. A. Aganbegyan, *The Economic Challenge of Perestroika* (Blooming-
    ton: Indiana University Press, 1988), p. 2.

58. Kostinsky and Belkindas, 'Official Soviet Gross National Product
    Accounting'.

59. The conference was titled 'Measuring Soviet GNP: Problems and
    Solutions', organized by the Directorate of Intelligence, CIA.

60. Cobb, Halstead and Rowe, 'If the GDP is Up, Why is America
    Down?', p. 6.

61. J. O'Neill, 'Building Better Global Economics BRICs', *Global Economics Paper* no. 66 (New York: Goldman Sachs, 2001).

62. 'Greenspan Sees Eventual Close of Gap in Workers' Incomes', *Los Angeles Times*, 8 April 1994.

63. P. Pierson and J.S. Hacker, *Winner-Take-All Politics: How Washington Made the Rich Richer – and Turned Its Back on the Middle Class* (New York: Simon & Schuster, 2010).

64. US Department of Commerce, 'GDP'.

65. William M. Daley, 'Press Conference Announcing the Department of Commerce's Achievement of the Century', 7 December 1999, in ibid., p. 10.

66. US Department of Commerce, 'GDP', p. 9.

67. Ibid.

68. 'Corporate Conduct: The President; Bush Signs Bill Aimed at Fraud in Corporations', *New York Times*, 31 July 2002.

69. 'The GDP Debate: Did a Recession Start in 2007?', *Wall Street Journal*, 31 July 2008.

70. 'How Did the Recent GDP Revisions Change the Picture of the 2007–2009 Recession and the Recovery?', Bureau of Economic Analysis, www.bea.gov/faq/index.cfm?faq_id=1004 (accessed May 2012).

71. J. Nalewayk, 'The Income- and Expenditure-Side Estimates of U.S. Output Growth', *Brookings Papers on Economic Activity*, Spring 2010: 71–127.

72. See www.bea.gov/newsreleases/national/gdp/gdpnewsrelease.htm (accessed 15 July 2012).

73. J.E. Stiglitz, A. Sen and J.-P. Fitoussi, (2009) *Report by the Commission on the Measurement of Economic Performance and Social Progress*, p. 8.

74. 'Economists Look to Expand GDP to Count "Quality of Life"', *New York Times*, 1 September 2008.

75. European Commission, *GDP and Beyond: Measuring Progress in a Changing World*, 2009, COM/2009/0433 final.

76. 'David Cameron Aims to Make Happiness the New GDP', *Guardian*, 14 November 2010.

77. 'Feds Want to Measure Gross National Happiness. Honest', *Washington Post*, 31 March 2012.

78. 'What's Wrong with GDP? The Attack on Economic Growth', *Fiscal Times*, 5 April 2012.

79. 'Ban: New Economic Paradigm Needed, Including Social and Environmental Progress', *UN News Centre*, 2 April 2012.

80. Quoted in US Department of Commerce, 'GDP', p. 9.

81. Cobb, Halstead and Rowe, 'If the GDP is Up, Why is America Down?', p. 6.

82. R. Higgs, 'The Cold War Economy: Opportunity Costs, Ideology, and the Politics of Crisis', Independent Institute, 1 July 1994, www.independent.org/publications/article.asp?id=1297 (accessed 15 July 2012).

CHAPTER 2

1. W.D. Nordhaus and J. Tobin, 'Is Growth Obsolete?', in M. Moss (ed.), *The Measurement of Economic and Social Performance*, special issue of *Studies in Income and Wealth*, vol. 38, 1973, p. 509.

2. Ibid.

3. The expression is used by Nordhaus and Tobin, 'Is Growth Obsolete?', p. 512.

4. A.B. Abel and B.S. Bernanke, *Macroeconomics* (New York: Pearson Addison Wesley, 2005).

5. E. Dickinson, 'GDP: A Brief History', *Foreign Policy*, January–February 2011.

6. Nordhaus and Tobin, 'Is Growth Obsolete?', p. 510.

7. W.J. Bennett, 'Quantifying America's Decline', *Wall Street Journal*, 15 March 1993.

8. Cited by W.J. Bennett, 'America at Risk: Can We Survive without Moral Values?', *USA Today*, November 1994: 14–16.

9. S. Kuznets, 'Quantitative Aspects of Economic Growth of Nations', special issue of *Economic Development and Cultural Changes* 5(1) (1956): 1–594.

10. S. Kuznets, *Shares of Upper Income Groups in Income and Saving* (New York: NBER, 1953).

11. OECD, *Growing Unequal: Income Distribution and Poverty in OECD Countries* (Paris: OECD, 2008); OECD, *Divided We Stand: Why Inequality Keeps Rising* (Paris: OECD, 2011).

12. E. Lundberg, 'Simon Kuznets' Contribution to Economics', *Swedish Journal of Economics* 73(4) (1971): 444–59.

13. S. Kuznets, 'How to Judge Quality', *New Republic*, 20 October 1962, p. 29.

14. S. Kuznets, *National Income and Capital Formation, 1919–1935* (New York: NBER, 1937), p. 3.

15. Ibid.

16. Ibid.

17. Nordhaus and Tobin, 'Is Growth Obsolete?', p. 513.

18. Quoted in 'Special Report: U.S. Data Dogs on Quest for Sexier

Statistics', Reuters, 6 July 2010.

19. S. Kuznets, *National Income – A Summary of Findings* (New York: National Bureau of Economic Research, 1946), p. 127.

20. Kuznets, *National Income and Capital Formation*, p. 6.

21. Ibid., p. 3.

22. Ibid., p. 5.

23. Ibid., p. 6.

24. Ibid.

25. Ibid., p. 5. See also S. Kuznets, 'National Income, 1919–1935', *NBER Bulletin* 66 (27 September 1937): 1–16.

26. Cited in J. Rowe, 'Our Phony Economy', *Harper's*, June 2008.

27. Kuznets, *National Income and Capital Formation*, p. 6.

28. As discussed in the Introduction, there are three ways to calculate GDP: the product (or output) approach, the income approach and the expenditure approach.

29. Kuznets, *National Income and Capital Formation*, p. 5.

30. Ibid.

31. Kuznets, *National Income – A Summary of Findings*, p. 127.

32. M. Abramovitz, 'The Welfare Interpretation of Secular Trends in National Income and Product', in M. Abramovitz et al. (eds), *The Allocation of Economic Resources: Essays in Honor of Bernard Francis Haley* (Oxford: Oxford University Press/Stanford, CA: Stanford University Press, 1959).

33. Ibid., p. 1.

34. Ibid., p. 5.

35. Nordhaus and Tobin, 'Is Growth Obsolete?', p. 515.

36. Ibid., p. 517.

37. C. Leipert, 'Social Costs of the Economic Process and National Accounts: The Example of Defensive Expenditures', *Journal of Interdisciplinary Economics* 3(2) (1989), p. 43. See also C. Leipert, 'National Income and Economic Growth: The Conceptual Side of Defensive Expenditures', *Journal of Economic Issues* 23(3) (1989): 851.

38. In 1937 Kuznets wrote: 'Moreover, the results of economic activity are evaluated at current market prices. These evaluations reflect, among other factors, inequalities in the distribution of income, differences among various types of service with respect to the competitive position of their producers, changes in the effective supply of money, and differences over space or time in the method of estimating the consumption of durable capital goods' (*National Income and Capital Formation*, pp. 6–7).

39. Abramovitz, 'The Welfare Interpretation of Secular Trends in

National Income and Product', p. 11.

40. Ibid., p. 11.

41. Ibid., p. 12.

42. Ibid., p.12.

43. R. Higgs, 'The Cold War Economy: Opportunity Costs, Ideology, and the Politics of Crisis', *Explorations in Economic History* 31(3) (1994): 283-312.

44. W.J. Baumol and W.G. Bowen, *Performing Arts: The Economic Dilemma* (Cambridge, MA: MIT Press, 1968).

45. M.J. Boskin et al., *Toward a More Accurate Measure of the Cost of Living: Final Report to the Senate Finance Committee* (Washington, DC: US Government Printing Office, 1996).

46. Stiglitz et al., *Report by the Commission on the Measurement of Economic Performance and Social Progress*, p. 23.

47. D. Wasshausen and B.R. Moulton, 'The Role of Hedonic Methods in Measuring Real GDP in the United States', paper presented at the 31st CEIES Seminar 'Are We Measuring Productivity Correctly?', organized by Eurostat, Rome, 12-13 October 2006.

48. A.W. Wyckoff, (1995) 'The Impact of Computer Prices on International Comparisons of Labour Productivity', *Economics of Innovation and New Technology* 3(3-4): 277-93. See also Eurostat Task Force, 'Volume Measures for Computers and Software', report of the Eurostat Task Force on Volume Measures for Computers and Software, June 1999.

49. Abramovitz, 'The Welfare Interpretation of Secular Trends in National Income and Product', p. 20.

50. Ibid., p. 14.

51. Ibid., p. 13.

52. Ibid., p. 15.

53. Ibid.

54. Ibid., p. 20.

55. A.J. Oswald, 'Happiness and Economic Performance', *Economic Journal* 107 (November 1997), p. 1827.

56. R.A. Easterlin, 'Does Economic Growth Improve the Human Lot? Some Empirical Evidence', in P.A. David and M.W. Reder (eds), *Nations and Households in Economic Growth: Essays in Honour of Moses Abramovitz* (New York and London: Academic Press, 1974), p. 121.

57. R. Easterlin, 'Will Raising the Income of All Increase the Happiness of All?', *Journal of Economic Behaviour and Organization* 27 (1995), pp. 35-6.

58. A. Maddison, *Dynamic Forces in Capitalist Development* (Oxford: Oxford University Press, 1991).

59. OECD, *Historical Statistics 1960–1990* (Paris: OECD, 1992).

60. R. Summers and A. Heston, 'The Penn World Table (Mark 5): An Expanded Set of International Comparisons, 1950–1988', *Quarterly Journal of Economics* 106(2) (1991): 327–68.

61. Y. Yasuba, 'Japan's Post-war Growth in Historical Perspective', *Japan Forum* 3 (April 1991): 57–70.

62. Easterlin, 'Will Raising the Income of All Increase the Happiness of All?'

63. Oswald, 'Happiness and Economic Performance', p. 1827.

64. Nordhaus and Tobin, 'Is Growth Obsolete?', p. 517.

65. K.A. Fox, (1973) 'Combining Economic and Non-economic Objectives in Development Planning: Problems of Concept and Measurement', US Agency for International Development, Occasional Paper 1, November 1973.

66. Nordhaus and Tobin, 'Is Growth Obsolete?', p. 520.

67. Kuznets, 'How to Judge Quality', p. 29.

68. Ibid.

69. See Nordhaus and Tobin, 'Is Growth Obsolete?'

70. Higgs, 'The Cold War Economy: Opportunity Costs, Ideology, and the Politics of Crisis'.

71. R. Higgs, 'Hard Coals Make Bad Law: Congressional Parochialism versus National Defense', *Cato Journal* 8 (1988): 79–106; C. Twight, 'Department of Defense Attempts to Close Military Bases: The Political Economy of Congressional Resistance', in R. Higgs (ed.), *Arms, Politics and the Economy: Historical and Contemporary Perspectives* (New York: Holmes & Meyer, 1990), pp. 236–80.

72. 'US Economic Growth Stronger in Q3', Reuters, 29 October 2005.

73. 'Breakups Alter Makeup of Housing Market', *Chicago Tribune*, 26 March 1995.

74. A.O. Hirschman, 'Rival Interpretations of the Market Society', *Journal of Economic Literature* 20 (December 1982), p. 1467.

75. See also A.O. Hirschmann, *The Strategy of Economic Development* (New Haven, CT: Yale University Press, 1968).

76. F. Hirsh, *Social Limits to Growth* (Cambridge, MA: Harvard University Press, 1976).

77. Ibid., p. 118.

78. K. Polanyi, *The Great Transformation: The Political and Economic Origins of Our Time* (Boston, MA: Beacon Press, 2001 [1944]).

79. A.M. Sievers, *The Mystical World of Indonesia: Culture and Economic Development in Conflict* (Baltimore, MD: Johns Hopkins University Press, 1974); N. Klein, *The Shock Doctrine: The Rise of Disaster Capitalism* (New York: Picador, 2008).

80. Hirsch, *Social Limits to Growth*. See also N. Shafik, 'Economic Development and Environmental Quality: An Econometric Analysis', *Oxford Economic Papers* 46 (1994): 757–73.

81. A. Antoci and S. Bartolini, 'Negative Externalities as the Engine of Growth in an Evolutionary Context', Working Paper No. 83/99, Fondazione ENI Enrico Mattei. 1999. See also S. Bartolini and L. Bonatti, 'Environmental and Social Degradation as the Engine of Economic Growth', *Ecological Economics* 41 (2002): 1–16.

82. Nordhaus and Tobin, 'Is Growth Obsolete?', p. 522.

83. Ibid.

84. R. Repetto et al., *Wasting Assets: Natural Resources in the National Income Accounts* (Washington, DC: World Resources Institute, 1989).

85. Their methodology was based on a model designed to understand the behaviour of complex systems. The model, called 'system dynamics', had been developed in the 1950s by MIT computer scientist Jay W. Forrester.

86. D. Meadows et al., *The Limits to Growth* (New York: Universe Books, 1972).

87. G. Nebbia, 'Bisogno di storia e di futuro', *Futuribili* 4(3) (1997): 149–82.

88. J.L Simon and H. Kahn (eds), *The Resourceful Earth: A Response to the Global 2000 Report* (New York: Basil Blackwell, 1984).

89. W.D. Nordhaus (1973) 'World Dynamics: Measurement without Data', *Economic Journal* 83(332) (1973): 1156–83; G. Myrdal, *Against the Stream: Critical Essays on Economics* (Pantheon Books, New York, 1973).

90. M. Jahoda, K.L.R. Pavitt, H.S.D Cole and C. Freeman (eds), *Models of Doom: A Critique of the Limits to Growth* (New York: Universe Publishing, 1973).

91. J.L. Simon, *The Ultimate Resource* (Princeton, NJ: Princeton University Press, 1981).

92. R. Bailey, 'Dr. Doom', *Forbes*, 16 October 1989, p. 45.

93. R. Golub and J. Townsend, 'Malthus, Multinationals and the Club of Rome', *Social Studies of Science* 7 (May 1977), p. 219.

94. U. Bardi, 'How "The Limits to Growth" Was Demonized', *The Oil Drum*, 9 March 2008; see also U. Bardi, *The Limits to Growth Revisited* (New York and Heidelberg: Springer, 2011)

95. W.D. Nordhaus, 'Lethal Model 2: The Limits to Growth Revisited', *Brookings Papers on Economic Activity* 23(2) (1992): 2.

96. Bardi, 'How "The Limits to Growth" Was Demonized'.

97. For a general analysis of conservative think-tanks' fight against

environmentalism from the publication of *Limits to Growth* until
2005, see P.J. Jacques, R.E. Dunlap and M. Freeman, 'The Organisation of Denial: Conservative Think Tanks and Environmental Scepticism', *Environmental Politics* 17(3) (2008): 349–85.

98. Bureau of Economic Analysis, 'Integrated Economic and Environmental Satellite Accounts', *Survey of Current Business* 74(4) (1994):
33–49.

99. Quoted in Easterlin, 'Does Economic Growth Improve the Human
Lot?', p. 121.

100. J.B. Schor, *The Overworked American: The Unexpected Decline of
Leisure* (New York: Basic Books, 1992), p. 1.

101. Nordhaus and Tobin, 'Is Growth Obsolete?', p. 512.

102. Kuznets, 'How to Judge Quality', p. 29.

103. Ibid., p. 31.

104. Speech by Robert F. Kennedy at the University of Kansas, 18 March
1968. Text available at the John F. Kennedy Presidential Library and
Museum.

CHAPTER 3

1. NEF, *The Happy Planet Index 2.0: Why Good Lives Don't Have to
Cost the Earth* (London: New Economics Foundation, 2009), p. 2.

2. World Commission on Environment and Development, *Our Common
Future* (Oxford: Oxford University Press, 1987), ch. 2.

3. Nordhaus and Tobin, 'Is Growth Obsolete?', p. 513.

4. Ibid., p. 513.

5. Ibid., p. 515.

6. Ibid., p. 513.

7. R. Eisner, *The Total Incomes System of Accounts* (Chicago: University
of Chicago Press, 1989), p. 9.

8. R. England, 'Alternatives to Gross National Product: A Critical Survey', in F. Ackerman et al. (eds), *Human Well-being and Economic
Goals* (Washington, DC: Island Press, 1998), pp. 373–402.

9. Eisner, *The Total Incomes System of Accounts*, p. 36.

10. 'Mixed Signals: Weaker Growth, Higher Profits', National Public
Radio, 27 April 2012.

11. England, 'Alternatives to Gross National Product', p. 382.

12. R. Ruggles, 'Review of the Total Incomes System of Accounts by
Robert Eisner', *Review of Income and Wealth* 37(4) (1991): 455–6.

13. H. Daly and J. Cobb, *For the Common Good: Redirecting the Economy toward Community, the Environment and a Sustainable Future*
(Boston, MA: Beacon Press, 1994).

14. Ibid., p. 445.
15. England, 'Alternatives to Gross National Product', p. 393.
16. Daly and Cobb, *For the Common Good*, p. 482.
17. S. Dietz and E. Neumayer, 'Some Constructive Criticisms of the Index of Sustainable Economic Welfare', in P. Lawn (ed.), *Sustainable Development Indicators and Ecological Economics* (Chetltenham: Edward Elgar, 2006), p. 189.
18. E. Neumayer, 'The ISEW – Not an Index of Sustainable Economic Welfare', *Social Indicators Research* 48(1) (1999): 77–101.
19. Ibid., p. 93.
20. England, 'Alternatives to Gross National Product', p. 388.
21. See www.socialwatch.org/node/11389 (accessed 15 July 2012).
22. See www.prosperity.com/summary.aspx (accessed 15 July 2012).
23. B. Ewing et al., *Ecological Footprint Atlas 2010* (Oakland, CA: Global Footprint Network, 2010).
24. NEF, *The Happy Planet Index 2.0*.
25. Whilst doing better than any other country, Costa Rica still exceeds its fair share of natural resources: it consumes 2.3 global hectares against a theoretical maximum allowance of 2.1 global hectares.
26. See GNH Index at www.grossnationalhappiness.com/articles (accessed 15 July 2012).
27. See www.grossnationalhappiness.com (accessed 15 July 2012).
28. S. Alkire and J. Foster, 'Counting and Multidimensional Poverty Measurement', *Journal of Public Economics* 95 (2011): 476–87.
29. Centre for Bhutan Studies, *Gross National Happiness Index Explained in Detail* (Thimpu: Centre for Bhutan Studies, 2011).
30. Ibid.
31. K.Ura, S. Alkire and T. Zangmo, *GNH and GNH Index* (Thimpu: Centre for Bhutan Studies, 2011).
32. For decades, Bhutanese citizens of Nepalese origins have been discriminated against in Bhutan and most of them have fled to Nepal as refugees. The Bhutan People's Party, the country's oldest political movement, was outlawed in the 1990s and was barred from contesting the country's first-ever elections held in 2008. Only two pro-monarchy parties were allowed to participate in the elections.
33. Act 113 of 8 May 2012.
34. A. White, 'A Global Projection of Subjective Well-being: A Challenge to Positive Psychology?' *Psychtalk* 56 (2007): 17–20.
35. 'Happiness: Toward a Holistic Approach to Development', UN General Assembly Resolution, A/65/L86, 25 August 2011.
36. World Bank, *World Development Report* (Washington, DC: World Bank, 1978), p. iii.

37. World Bank, *World Development Report* (Oxford: Oxford University Press, 1994), pp. 157, 230.

38. This indicator was introduced by D.W. Pearce and G.D. Atkinson, 'Capital Theory and the Measurement of Weak Sustainable Development: An Indicator of Weak Sustainability', *Ecological Economics* 8 (1993): 103–8.

39. World Bank, *Where is the Wealth of Nations? Measuring Capital for the 21st Century* (Washington, DC: World Bank, 2006), p. XVI.

40. UNDP, *Human Development Report 1990* (New York: Oxford University Press, 1990), p. 9.

41. UNDP, *Human Development Report 1994* (New York: Oxford University Press, 1994), p. 91.

42. J. Gertner, 'The Rise and Fall of the GDP', *New York Times* magazine, 13 May 2010.

43. P. Dagupta and M. Weale, 'On Measuring the Quality of Life', *World Development* 20(1) (1992): 119–31.

44. B. Caplan, 'Against the Human Development Index', *Library of Economics and Liberty*, 22 May 2009, http://econlog.econlib.org/archives/2009/05/against_the_hum.html (accessed 15 July 2012).

45. See the methodological note at http://hdr.undp. org/en/statistics/ihdi (accessed 15 July 2012).

46. 'Going Beyond GDP: UNDP Proposes Human Development Measure of Sustainability', *PRWeb*, 20 June 2012, www.prweb.com/releases/2012/6/prweb9623323.htm (accessed 15 July 2012).

47. J.E. Stiglitz, A. Sen and J.-P. Fitoussi, *Report by the Commission on the Measurement of Economic Performance and Social Progress* (2009), www.stiglitz-se-fitoussi.fr, p. 15.

48. Ibid., p. 17.

49. Ibid.

50. OECD, *How's Life? Measuring Well-Being* (Paris: OECD, 2011).

51. See http://oecdbetterlifeindex.org (accessed 15 July 2012).

52. Gertner, 'The Rise and Fall of the GDP'.

53. Ibid.

54. Ibid.

55. V. Miranda, 'Cooking, Caring and Volunteering: Unpaid Work around the World', *OECD Social, Employment and Migration Working Papers* No. 116 (Paris: OECD, 2011).

56. 'Green GDP System to Debut in 3–5 years in China', *People's Daily Online*, 12 March 2004, http://english.people.com.cn/200403/11/eng 20040311_137244.shtml (accessed 15 July 2012).

57. 'Green GDP Accounting Study Report 2004 Issues', www.gov.cn/english/2006-09/11/content_384596.htm (accessed 15 July 2012).

58. 'Green GDP System to Debut in 3–5 Years in China'.
59. 'China Issues First "Green GDP" Report', *China Dialogue*, 7 September 2006.
60. 'Green GDP in the Works', *China Daily*, 23 July 2011.
61. 'Green GDP Accounting Study Report 2004 Issues'.
62. 'A Courageous Voice for a Greener China', *Bloomberg Businessweek*, 11 July 2005.
63. M. Liu, 'Where Poor is a Poor Excuse', *Newsweek*, 28 June 2008.
64. 'The Man Making China Green', *New Statesman*, December 2006–January 2007, pp. 60–61.
65. J.Y Kim et al., *Dying for Growth: Global Inequality and the Health of the Poor* (Monroe, ME: Common Courage Press, 2002), p. 7.
66. 'Hats Off to Ngozi', *The Economist*, 31 March 2012.
67. 'US World Bank Nominee Under Fire Over Book', *Financial Times*, 26 March 2012.
68. 'Obama Nominee for World Bank President Takes His Cue from Noam Chomsky', *The American*, 26 March 2012.
69. J.Y. Kim, 'My Call for an Open, Inclusive World Bank', *Financial Times*, 28 March 2012.
70. UN et al., *System of National Accounts 1993* (Brussels/Luxembourg, New York, Paris, Washington DC: UN, World Bank, International Monetary Fund, European Commission, OECD, 1993).
71. D. Blades, 'Revision of the System of National Accounts: A Note on Objectives and Key Issues', *OECD Economic Studies* 12 (Paris: OECD, 1989), p. 214.
72. Ibid., p. 215.
73. UN et al., *System of National Accounts 2008* (Brussels/Luxembourg, New York, Paris, Washington DC: UN, World Bank, International Monetary Fund, European Commission, OECD, 2008), p. 7.
74. Ibid., p. 7.
75. SIPRI, *Background Paper on SIPRI Military Expenditure Data, 2011* (Stockholm: SIPRI, 2012).
76. Gertner, 'The Rise and Fall of the GDP'.
77. 'What's Wrong with GDP? An Attack on Economic Growth', *The Fiscal Times*, 5 April 2012.
78. See www.nationalaccountsofwellbeing.org (accessed 15 July 2012).
79. 'Speech on Wellbeing', transcript of a speech given by the prime minister on well-being on 25 November 2010, www.number10.gov.uk/news/pm-speech-on-well-being (accessed 15 July 2012).
80. H. Daly, *The Steady State Economy* (London: W.H. Freeman, 1972), p. 119.
81. 'UK to Press for Global Green Accounting System', *Independent*, 10

February 2012. See also 'GDP Plus: Nick Clegg Announces UK Natural Capital Will Be Measured and Urges Others to Do the Same', *Information Daily*, 23 June 2012, www.egovmonitor.com/node/51507 (accessed 15 July 2012).

82. See www.ihdp. unu.edu/article/iwr (accessed 15 July 2012).

83. For more information, see www.wavespartnership. org (accessed 15 July 2012).

84. D. Pearce, A. Markandya and E. Barbier, *Blueprint for a Green Economy* (London: Earthscan, 1989), p. 81.

85. The principle of weak sustainability is generally known in economics as the Hartwick's rule, which defines the amount of investment in produced capital that is necessary to offset declining stocks of non-renewable resources. This approach has informed, among others, a number of estimates of 'genuine saving' produced by the World Bank.

86. Besides a number of institutions belonging to the World Bank Group, signatories of the Natural Capital Declaration include private banks such as China Merchants Bank, Standard Chartered and Unicredit. See www.naturalcapitaldeclaration.org (accessed 15 July 2012).

87. 'Beyond GDP: Measuring What Really Matters to our Prosperity and Future', Greenpeace International, July 2012.

88. E.F. Schumacher, *Small is Beautiful: A Study of Economics As If People Mattered* (London: Vintage, 1973), p. 31.

CHAPTER 4

1. 'Argentina: The Post-Money Economy', *Time*, 5 February 2002.

2. Currently, the *red global de trueque* (Global Network of Barter) is the most widespread barter community in Argentina and publishes an online magazine focused on economic self-sufficiency, *Autosuficiencia Economica* (www.autosuficiencia.com.ar).

3. B. Rossmeissl, 'El trueque en Argentina: estrategia eficiente en tiempo de crisis', *Observatorio de La Economia Latinoamericana* 37 (2005), www.eumed.net/cursecon/ecolat/ar/2005/br-trueque.htm (accessed 15 July 2012).

4. R. Pearson, 'Argentina's Barter Network: New Currency for New Times?', *Bulletin of Latin American Research* 22(2) (2003): 214–30.

5. P. Ould-Ahmed, 'Can a Community Currency Be Independent of the State Currency? A Case Study of the Credito in Argentina', *Environment and Planning* 42 (2010): 1346–64.

6. On 22 August 2000, the GIP-Metal became the first factory to be repossessed by its dismissed employees. Over time these instances have

multiplied, giving birth to a fully fledged movement, the Movimiento Nacional de Fabricas Recuperadas por los Trabajadores.

7. A.L. Abramovich and G. Vázquez, 'La experiencia del trueque en la Argentina: otro mercado es possible', Central de Trabajadores Argentinos, Instituto de Estudios y Formación, *Seminario de Economía Social*, 2003, pp. 23–61.

8. For a description of the struggle between official and alternative economies in Argentina, see the film documentary *Trueque* (Barter), released in 2008.

9. Permaculture is a systematic method that was first coined by Australians Bill Mollison and David Holmgren during the 1970s. The word 'permaculture' originally referred to 'permanent agriculture' but was expanded to include all forms of 'culture', given that social aspects are integral to a truly sustainable system.

10. R. Hopkins, *Kinsale 2021: An Energy Descendent Action Plan* (Kinsale: Kinsale Further Education College, 2005), p. 3.

11. Ibid.

12. These sections are based on a series of conversations I had with Rob Hopkins in May/June 2012.

13. R. Hopkins, *The Transition Handbook: from Oil Dependency to Local Resilience* (Totnes: Green Books, 2008).

14. See www.transitiontowntotnes.org (accessed 15 July 2012).

15. As an example, see the initiative Atmos Totnes. More details at www.atmostotnes.org (accessed 17 May 2012).

16. M.K. Hubbert, 'Nuclear Energy and the Fossil Fuels', paper presented before the Spring Meeting of the Southern District, Division of Production, American Petroleum Institute, Publication 95 (San Antonio, Texas: Shell Development, 1956).

17. See www.eia.gov/dnav/pet/hist/LeafHandler.ashx?n=PET&s=MCRFPUS2&f=A (accessed 15 July 2012).

18. 'Has the World Already Passed "Peak Oil"?', *National Geographic*, 9 November 2010; 'Is Peak Oil Behind Us?', *New York Times*, 14 November 2010.

19. Conversation with Rob Hopkins, 14 June 2012.

20. Further details about their community energy projects can be found at www.bwce.coop, www.brixtonenergy.co.uk, www.tresoc.co.uk (accessed 15 July 2012).

21. V. Lebow, 'Price Competition in 1955', *Journal of Retailing* 31(1) (Spring 1955): 5–10.

22. See www.transitionnetwork.org/support/what-transition-initiative (accessed 15 July 2012).

23. 'The End is Near! (Yay!)', *New York Times*, 16 April 2009.

24. Conversation with Rob Hopkins, 14 June 2012.
25. P. Chatterton and A. Cutler, *The Rocky Road to a Real Transition: The Transition Towns Movement and What It Means for Social Change*, online publication of the Trapese Collective (2008), www.trapese. org, p. 6.
26. See Hopkins's response 'To Ted Trainer's Friendly Criticism of Transition', http://transitionculture.org/2009/09/08/responding-to-ted-trainers-friendly-criticism-of-transition (accessed 15 July 2012). See also 'What's Next for Transition Towns?', *Guardian*, 28 May 2009.
27. 'The Rocky Road to a Real Transition: A Review', *Transition Culture* blog, 25 May 2008, www.transitionculture.org (accessed 15 July 2012).
28. This is the official definition provided on www.degrowth.org (accessed 15 July 2012). I wish to thank Federico Demaria of Research and Degrowth at the Universitat Autònoma de Barcelona for his comments to this chapter.
29. N. Georgescu-Roegen, *The Entropy Law and the Economic Process* (Cambridge, MA: Harvard University Press, 1971).
30. P. Victor, *Managing Without Growth: Slower by Design, Not Disaster* (Northampton, MA: Edward Elgar, 2008).
31. D. Belpomme, *Avant qu'il ne soit trop tard* (Paris: Fayard, 2007).
32. S. Latouche, *Farewell to Growth* (Cambridge: Polity Press, 2009), p. 55.
33. Ibid., pp. 33ff.
34. M. Bookchin, *Toward an Ecological Society* (Montreal: Black Rose Books, 1980); G. Esteva and M.S. Prakash, *Grassroots Postmodernism: Remaking the Soil of Cultures* (London: Zed Books, 1998); A. Magnaghi, 'Dalla città metropolitana alla (bio)regione urbana', in A. Marson (ed.), *Il Progetto di Territorio nella Città Metropolitana* (Florence: Alinea, 2006).
35. Conversation with Rob Hopkins, 29 May 2012.
36. T. Jackson, *Prosperity without Growth: Economics for a Finite Planet* (London: Earthscan, 2009), p. 188.
37. NEF, *The Great Transition* (London: New Economics Foundation, 2009), www.neweconomics.org/publications/great-transition (accessed 15 July 2012).
38. 'Printer Rolling in Back Notes', *This is Plymouth*, 30 August 2008.
39. 'The Rocky Road to a Real Transition: A Review', *Transition Culture* blog, 25 May 2008, www.transitionculture.org (accessed 15 July 2012).
40. Conversation with Rob Hopkins, 29 May 2012. See also the animation

'Leaky Bucket' in the film *In Transition 2.0.*

41. 'No Money? Then Make Your Own', *BBC News*, 17 September 2009.

42. See www.bristolpound.org (accessed 15 July 2012).

43. R.F.H. Schroeder, Y. Miyazaki and M. Fare, 'Community Currency Research: An Analysis of the Literature', *International Journal of Community Currency Research* 15 (2011): 31–41.

44. See www.sol-reseau.org (accessed 15 July 2012).

45. For more information, see www.ovolos.gr (accessed 15 July 2012).

46. 'Battered by Economic Crisis, Greeks Turn to Barter Networks', *New York Times*, 1 October 2011.

47. See www.regiogeld.de (accessed 15 July 2012).

48. 'Rival to Euro as Germans Cash in on Currency', *Telegraph*, 29 January 2007.

49. 'Alternative Currencies Flourishing in Germany', *New American*, 24 May 2010.

50. Ibid.

51. P. Hawken, *Blessed Unrest. How the Largest Social Movement in History Is Restoring Grace, Justice, and Beauty to the World* (London: Penguin, 2007), p. 190.

52. S. Latouche, *Farewell to Growth* (Cambridge: Polity Press, 2009), p. 9.

53. L.R. Brown, *Plan B 4.0 – Mobilizing to Save Civilization* (London and New York: W.W. Norton, 2009), p. 259.

CONCLUSION

1. K.E. Boulding, 'The Economics of the Coming Spaceship Earth', in H. Jarrett (ed.), *Environmental Quality in a Growing Economy* (Baltimore, MD: Resources for the Future/Johns Hopkins University Press, 1966), pp. 3–14.

2. K. Rogoff, 'Rethinking the Growth Imperative', *Project Syndicate*, 2 January 2012.

3. I. Janis, *Victims of Groupthink* (New York: Houghton Mifflin, 1972). I owe the reference to groupthink to one of my students, who used it as an explanatory variable in the analysis of policy disasters.

4. Ibid.

5. T. Judt, *Ill Fares the Land: A Treatise on Our Present Discontents* (London: Penguin, 2010), p. 157.

6. See, for instance, *In Debt We Trust*, the prescient documentary by Danny Schechter released in 2006.

7. 'Queen Told How Economists Missed Financial Crisis', *Telegraph*,

26 July 2009.
8. P. Krugman, 'How did Economists Get It So Wrong', *New York Times* magazine, 2 September 2009.
9. Janis, *Victims of Groupthink.*
10. S. Kuznets, *National Income and Its Composition (1919–1938)*, Vol. I (New York: NBER, 1941), p. 5.
11. S. Latouche, *Farewell to Growth* (Cambridge: Polity Press, 2009), p. 19.
12. C. Lindblom, 'The Market as a Prison', *Journal of Politics* 44 (1982): 325–6.
13. P. Kennedy, *The Rise and Fall of the Great Powers* (London: Vintage, 1989).
14. See http://ec.europa.eu/europe2020/index_en.htm (accessed 15 July 2012).
15. The Ponzi scheme is a fraudulent investment operation that pays returns to investors out of their own money or out of the money made available by subsequent investors. As it is not based on any real profit, the scheme requires an ever-growing level of investment and ultimately collapses when the promoter vanishes with the money or when total invested capital runs dry.
16. Latouche, *Farewell to Growth*, p. 8.
17. N.D. Kristof and S. WuDunn, *Thunder from the East: Portrait of a Rising Asia* (New York: Knopf, 2000) .
18. Lindblom, 'The Market as a Prison', p. 332.
19. Ibid., p. 330.

Bibliography

Abel, A.B., and Bernanke, B.S. (2005) *Macroeconomics* (New York: Pearson Addison Wesley).

Abramovich, A.L., and Vázquez, G. (2003) 'La experiencia del trueque en la Argentina: otro mercado es possible', *Central de Trabajadores Argentinos, Instituto de Estudios y Formación, Seminario de Economía Social*, pp. 23–61.

Abramovitz, M. (1959) 'The Welfare Interpretation of Secular Trends in National Income and Product', in M. Abramovitz et al. (eds), *The Allocation of Economic Resources: Essays in Honor of Bernard Francis Haley* (Oxford: Oxford University Press/Stanford, CA: Stanford University Press).

Aganbegyan, A. (1988) *The Economic Challenge of Perestroika* (Bloomington: Indiana University Press).

Alkire, S., and Foster, J. (2011) 'Counting and Multidimensional Poverty Measurement', *Journal of Public Economics* 95: 476–87.

Antoci, A., and Bartolini, S. (1999) 'Negative Externalities as the Engine of Growth in an Evolutionary Context', *Working Paper* no. 83/99, Fondazione ENI Enrico Mattei.

Bailey, R. (1989) 'Dr. Doom', *Forbes*, 16 October, p. 45.

Bardi, U. (2008) 'How "The Limits to Growth" Was Demonized', *The Oil Drum*, 9 March.

Bardi, U. (2011) *The Limits to Growth Revisited* (New York and Heidelberg: Springer).

Bartolini, S., and Bonatti, L. (2002) 'Environmental and Social Degradation as the Engine of Economic Growth', *Ecological Economics* 41: 1–16.

Baumol, W. J., and Bowen, W.G. (1968) *Performing Arts: The Economic Dilemma* (Cambridge, MA: MIT Press).

Belpomme, D. (2007) *Avant qu'il ne soit trop tard* (Paris: Fayard).

Bennett, W.J. (1993) 'Quantifying America's Decline', *Wall Street Journal*, 15 March.

Bennett, W.J. (1994) 'America at Risk: Can We Survive without Moral Values?', *USA Today* magazine, November: 14–16.

Blades, D. (1989) 'Revision of the System of National Accounts: A Note on Objectives and Key Issues', *OECD Economic Studies*, No. 12 (Paris: OECD).

Bookchin, M. (1980) *Toward and Ecological Society* (Montreal: Black Rose Books).

Boretsky, M. (1987) 'The Tenability of the CIA's Estimates of Soviet Economic Growth', *Journal of Comparative Economics* 11: 517–42.

Boskin, M.J., et al. (1996) *Toward a More Accurate Measure of the Cost of Living: Final Report to the Senate Finance committee* (Washington, DC: US Government Printing Office).

Boulding, K.E. (1966) 'The Economics of the Coming Spaceship Earth', in H. Jarrett (ed.), *Environmental Quality in a Growing Economy* (Baltimore, MD: Resources for the Future/Johns Hopkins University Press).

Brown, L.R. (2009) *Plan B 4.0 – Mobilizing to Save Civilization* (London and New York: W.W. Norton).

Bureau of Economic Analysis (1994) 'Integrated Economic and Environmental Satellite Accounts', *Survey of Current Business* 74(4): 33–49.

Bureau of Economic Analysis (2007) *Measuring the Economy: A Primer on GDP and the National Income and Product Accounts* (Washington, DC: Department of Commerce).

Canny, N. (1987) *From Reformation to Resistance: Ireland, 1534–1660* (Dublin: Helicon).

Caplan, B. (2009) 'Against the Human Development Index', Library of Economics and Liberty blog, 22 May 2009, http://econlog.econlib.org/archives/2009/05/against_the_hum.html (accessed 15 July 2012).

Carlyle, T. (1850) 'The Present Time', *Latter Day Pamphlets*, Issue 1, February.

Carson, C.S. (1975) 'The History of the United States National Income and

Product Accounts: The Development of an Analytical Tool', *Review of Income and Wealth* 21(2): 153–81.

Carson, C.S. (1991) 'The Conference on Research in Income and Wealth: The Early Years', in Ernst R. Berndt and Jack E. Triplett (eds), *Fifty Years of Economic Measurement: The Jubilee of the Conference on Research in Income and Wealth* (Chicago: University of Chicago Press).

Centre for Bhutan Studies (2011) *Gross National Happiness Index Explained in Detail* (Thimpu: Centre for Bhutan Studies).

Cobb, C., Halstead, T., and Rowe, K. (1995) 'If the GDP is Up, Why is America Down?', *Atlantic Monthly*, October 1995, www.theatlantic.com/past/politics/ecbig/gdp. htm (accessed 15 July 2012).

Dagupta, P., and Weale, M. (1992) 'On Measuring the Quality of Life', *World Development* 20(1): 119–31.

Daly, H. (1972) *The Steady State Economy* (London: W.H. Freeman).

Daly, H., and Cobb, J. (1994) *For the Common Good: Redirecting the Economy toward Community, the Environment and a Sustainable Future* (Boston, MA: Beacon Press).

Demos (2012) *Beyond GDP: New Measures for a New Economy* (Demos: New York).

Dickinson, E. (2011) 'GDP: A Brief History', *Foreign Policy*, January–February.

Dietz, S., and Neumayer, E. (2006) 'Some Constructive Criticisms of the Index of Sustainable Economic Welfare', in P. Lawn (ed.), *Sustainable Development Indicators and Ecological Economics* (Chetltenham: Edward Elgar).

Easterlin, R.A. (1974) 'Does Economic Growth Improve the Human Lot? Some Empirical Evidence', in P.A. David and M.. Reder (eds), *Nations and Households in Economic Growth: Essays in Honour of Moses Abramovitz* (New York and London: Academic Press).

Easterlin R.A. (1995) 'Will Raising the Income of All Increase the Happiness of All?', *Journal of Economic Behaviour and Organization* 27: 35–47.

Eisner, R. (1989) *The Total Incomes System of Accounts* (Chicago: University of Chicago Press).

England, R. (1998) 'Alternatives to Gross National Product: A Critical Survey', in F. Ackerman et al. (eds), *Human Well-being and Economic Goals* (Washington DC: Island Press)

Ericson, R.E. (1988) 'The Soviet Statistical Debate: Khanin vs. TsSU', paper presented at Hoover–Rand Conference, Stanford University, March 1988.

Esteva, G., and Prakash, M.S. (1998) *Grassroots Postmodernism: Remaking the Soil of Cultures* (London: Zed Books).

European Commission (2009) *GDP and Beyond: Measuring Progress in a Changing World*, COM/2009/0433 final.

Eurostat Task Force (1999) 'Volume Measures for Computers and Software', report of the Eurostat Task Force on Volume Measures for Computers and Software, June.

Ewing, B., et al. (2010) *Ecological Footprint Atlas 2010* (Oakland, CA: Global Footprint Network).

Foertsch, T. (2006) 'A Victory for Taxpayers and the Economy', Heritage Foundation, WebMemo#1082, www.heritage.org/research/reports/2006/05/a-victory-for-taxpayers-and-the-economy (accessed 15 July 2012).

Fox, K.A. (1973) 'Combining Economic and Non-economic Objectives in Development Planning: Problems of Concept and Measurement', US Agency for International Development *Occasional Paper* 1, November.

Galbraith, J.K. (1980) 'The National Accounts: Arrival and Impact', in N. Cousins (ed.), *Reflections of America: Commemorating the Statistical Abstract Centennial* (Washington, DC: US Department of Commerce, Bureau of the Census).

Georgescu-Roegen, N. (1971) *The Entropy Law and the Economic Process* (Cambridge, MA: Harvard University Press).

Gertner, J. (2010) 'The Rise and Fall of the GDP', *New York Times* magazine, 13 May.

Golub, R., and Townsend, J. (1977) 'Malthus, Multinationals and the Club of Rome', *Social Studies of Science* 7 (May): 201–22.

Gorbunov, E.P. (1970) 'The Gross Social Product', translated in A.M. Prokhorov (ed.), *Great Soviet Encyclopaedia* (New York: Macmillan/London: Collier Macmillan, 1974–83).

Hawken, P. (2007) *Blessed Unrest: How the Largest Social Movement in History Is Restoring Grace, Justice, and Beauty to the World* (London: Penguin).

Higgs, R. (1988) 'Hard Coals Make Bad Law: Congressional Parochialism versus National Defense', *Cato Journal* 8: 79–106.

Higgs, R. (1992) 'Wartime Prosperity? A Reassessment of the US Economy in the 1940s', *Journal of Economic History* 52(1): 41–60.

Higgs, R. (1994) 'The Cold War Economy: Opportunity Costs, Ideology, and the Politics of Crisis', *Explorations in Economic History* 31(3): 283–312.

Hirsch, F. (1976) *Social Limits to Growth* (Cambridge, MA: Harvard University Press).

Hirschmann, A.O (1968) *The Strategy of Economic Development* (New Haven, CT: Yale University Press).

Hirschman, A.O. (1982) 'Rival Interpretations of the Market Society', *Journal of Economic Literature* 20 (December): 1463–84.

Hopkins, R. (2005) *Kinsale 2021: An Energy Descendent Action Plan* (Kinsale: Kinsale Further Education College).

Hopkins, R. (2008) *The Transition Handbook: From Oil Dependency to Local Resilience* (Totnes: Green Books).

Hubbert, M.K. (1956) 'Nuclear Energy and the Fossil Fuels', paper presented before the Spring Meeting of the Southern District, Division of Production, American Petroleum Institute, Publication 95 (San Antonio, TX: Shell Development Company).

IPCC (2000) *Emissions Scenarios* (Cambridge: Cambridge University Press).

Jackson, T. (2009) *Prosperity without Growth: Economics for a Finite Planet* (London: Earthscan).

Jacques, P.J., Dunlap, R.E., and Freeman, M. (2008) 'The Organisation of Denial: Conservative Think Tanks and Environmental Scepticism', *Environmental Politics* 17(3): 349–85.

Jahoda, M., Pavitt, K.L.R., Cole, H.S.D., and Freeman C. (1973) (eds) *Models of Doom: A Critique of the Limits to Growth* (New York: Universe).

Janis, I. (1972) *Victims of Groupthink* (New York: Houghton Mifflin).

Judt, T. (2010) *Ill Fares the Land: A Treatise on Our Present Discontents* (London: Penguin)

Kapuria-Foreman, V., and Perlman, M. (1995) 'An Economic Historian's Economist: Remembering Simon Kuznets', *Economic Journal* 105 (433): 1524–47.

Kennedy, P. (1989) *The Rise and Fall of the Great Powers* (London: Vintage).

Khomenko, T.A. (2006) 'Estimation of Gross Social Product and Net Material Product in the USSR', Discussion Paper Series no. 172, Institute for Economic Research, Hitotsubashi University, Tokyo, July.

Kim, J.Y. (2012) 'My Call for an Open, Inclusive World Bank', *Financial Times*, 28 March.

Kim, J.Y., et al. (2002) *Dying for Growth: Global Inequality and the Health of the Poor* (Monroe, ME: Common Courage Press).

Klein, N. (2008) *The Shock Doctrine: The Rise of Disaster Capitalism* (New York: Picador).

Kostinsky, B., and Belkindas, M. (1990) 'Official Soviet Gross National Product Accounting', in *Measuring Soviet GNP: Problems and Solutions*, report from conference sponsored by CIA Office of Soviet Analysis.

Kristof, N.D., and WuDunn, S. (2000) *Thunder from the East: Portrait of a Rising Asia* (New York: Knopf).

Krugman, P. (2009) 'How did Economists Get It So Wrong', *New York Times* magazine, 2 September.

Kushnirsky, F. (1988) 'New Challenges to Soviet Official Statistics: A Methodological Survey', in *The Impact of Gorbachev's Policies on Soviet Economic Statistics*, report from the conference sponsored by the CIA's Office of Soviet Analysis, pp. 11–26.

Kuznets, S. (1934) 'National Income, 1929–1932, *NBER Bulletin* 49, 7 June.

Kuznets, S. (1937) 'National Income, 1919–1935', *NBER Bulletin* 66, 27 September.

Kuznets, S. (1937) *National Income and Capital Formation, 1919–1935* (New York: National Bureau of Economic Research).

Kuznets, S. (1941) *National Income and Its Composition (1919–1938)*, Vol. I (New York: NBER).

Kuznets, S. (1946) *National Income – A Summary of Findings* (New York: National Bureau of Economic Research).

Kuznets, S. (1951) 'Government Product and National Income', in E. Lundberg (ed.), *Income and Wealth* (Cambridge: Cambridge University Press).

Kuznets, S. (1953) *Shares of Upper Income Groups in Income and Saving* (New York: NBER).

Kuznets, S. (1956) 'Quantitative Aspects of Economic Growth of Nations', special issue of *Economic Development and Cultural Changes* 5(1): 1–594.

Kuznets, S. (1962) 'How to Judge Quality', *New Republic*, 20 October.

Lacey, J. (2011) *Keep from All Thoughtful Men: How US Economists Won World War Two* (Annapolis, MD: Naval Institute Press).

Latouche, S. (2009) *Farewell to Growth* (Cambridge: Polity Press).

Lebow, V. (1955) 'Price Competition in 1955', *Journal of Retailing* 31(1) (Spring): 5–10.

Leipert, C. (1989) 'National Income and Economic Growth: The Conceptual Side of Defensive Expenditures', *Journal of Economic Issues* 23(3): 843–56.

Leipert, C. (1989) 'Social Costs of the Economic Process and National Accounts: The Example of Defensive Expenditures', *Journal of Interdisciplinary Economics* 3(2): 27–46.

Lindblom, C. (1982) 'The Market as a Prison', *Journal of Politics* 44: 324–36.

Lundberg, E. (1971) 'Simon Kuznets' Contribution to Economics', *Swedish Journal of Economics* 73(4): 444–59.

Maddison, A. (1991) *Dynamic Forces in Capitalist Development* (Oxford: Oxford University Press).

Magnaghi, A. (2006) 'Dalla città metropolitana alla (bio)regione urbana', in A. Marson (ed.), *Il Progetto di Territorio nella Città Metropolitana* (Florence: Alinea).

Marx, K. ([1885] 1909) *Capital: A Critique of Political Economy*, Vol. II: *The Process of Circulation of Capital* (Chicago: C.H. Kerr).

Meadows, D., et al. (1972) *The Limits to Growth* (New York: Universe).

Miranda, V. (2011) 'Cooking, Caring and Volunteering: Unpaid Work around the World', *OECD Social, Employment and Migration Working Papers*, No. 116 (Paris: OECD).

Myrdal, G. (1973) *Against the Stream: Critical Essays on Economics* (New York: Pantheon Books).

Nalewayk, J. (2010) 'The Income- and Expenditure-Side Estimates of U.S. Output Growth', *Brookings Papers on Economic Activity*, Spring: 71–127.

Nathan, R. (1994) 'GNP and Military Mobilization', *Journal of Evolutionary Economics* 4(1): 1–16.

NBER (1939) *Studies in Income and Wealth*, Vol. III (New York: National Bureau of Economic Research).

NBER (1946) *Studies in Income and Wealth* (New York: National Bureau of Economic Research).

Nebbia, G. (1997) 'Bisogno di storia e di futuro', *Futuribili* 4(3): 149–82.

NEF (2009) *The Great Transition* (London: New Economics Foundation).

NEF (2009) *The Happy Planet Index 2.0: Why Good Lives Don't Have To Cost the Earth* (London: New Economics Foundation).

Neumayer, E. (1999) 'The ISEW – Not an Index of Sustainable Economic Welfare', *Social Indicators Research* 48(1): 77–101.

Nordhaus W.D. (1973) 'World Dynamics: Measurement without Data', *Economic Journal* 83(332): 1156–83;

Nordhaus W.D. (1992) 'Lethal Model 2: The Limits to Growth Revisited', *Brookings Papers on Economic Activity* 23(2): 2.

Nordhaus, W.D., and Tobin, J. (1971) 'Is Growth Obsolete?', reprinted from Moss. M. (ed.), *The Measurement of Economic and Social Performance*, special issue of *Studies in Income and Wealth* 38: 509–32.

Noren, J.H. (2003) 'CIA's Analysis of the Soviet Economy', in G.K. Haines and R.E. Leggett (eds), *Watching the Bear: Essays on CIA's Analysis of the Soviet Union* (Washington, DC: Central Intelligence Agency).

OECD (1992) *Historical Statistics 1960–1990* (Paris: OECD).

OECD (2008) *Growing Unequal: Income Distribution and Poverty in OECD Countries* (Paris: OECD).

OECD (2008) *Statistics, Policy and Knowledge 2007: Measuring and Fostering the Progress of Societies* (Paris, OECD).

OECD (2011) *Divided We Stand: Why Inequality Keeps Rising* (Paris: OECD).

OECD (2011) *How's Life? Measuring Well-Being* (Paris: OECD).

O'Neill, J. (2001) 'Building Better Global Economics BRICs', *Global Economics Paper* no. 66 (New York: Goldman Sachs).

Oswald, A.J. (1997) 'Happiness and Economic Performance', *Economic Journal* 107 (November): 1815–31.

Ould-Ahmed, P. (2010) 'Can a Community Currency Be Independent of the State Currency? A Case Study of the Credito in Argentina', *Environment and Planning* 42: 1346–64.

Pearce, D., Markandya, A., and Barbier, E. (1989) *Blueprint for a Green Economy* (London: Earthscan).

Pearce, D.W., and Atkinson, G.D. (1993) 'Capital Theory and the Measurement of Weak Sustainable Development: An Indicator of Weak Sustainability', *Ecological Economics* 8: 103–8.

Pearson, R. (2003) 'Argentina's Barter Network: New Currency for New Times?', *Bulletin of Latin American Research* 22(2): 214–30.

Petty, W. (1986) The Economic Writings of Sir William Petty (Fairfield, NJ: Augustus M. Kelley).

Pierson, P., and Hacker, J.S. (2010) *Winner-Take-All Politics: How Washington Made the Rich Richer – and Turned Its Back on the Middle Class* (New York: Simon & Schuster).

Polanyi, K. (2001 [1944]) *The Great Transformation: The Political and Economic Origins of Our Time* (Boston, MA: Beacon Press).

Poovey, M. (1998) *A History of the Modern Fact* (Chicago and London: University of Chicago Press).

Repetto, R., et al. (1989) *Wasting Assets: Natural Resources in the National Income Accounts* (Washington, DC: World Resources Institute).

Rogoff, K. (2012) 'Rethinking the Growth Imperative', *Project Syndicate*, 2 January 2012, www.project-syndicate.org/commentary/rethinking-the-growth-imperative (accessed 15 July 2012).

Roncaglia, A. (1985) *Petty: The Origins of Political Economy* (Armonk, NY: M.E. Sharpe).

Rossmeissl, B. (2005) 'El trueque en Argentina: estrategia eficiente en tiempo de crisis', Observatorio de La Economia Latinoamericana, 37. Available at www.eumed.net/cursecon/ecolat/ar/2005/br-trueque.htm (accessed 15 July 2012).

Rowe, J. (2008) 'Our Phony Economy', *Harper's*, June.

Ruggles, R. (1991) 'Review of the Total Incomes System of Accounts by Robert Eisner', *Review of Income and Wealth* 37(4): 455–60.

Schneider, F., and Enste, D. (2002) 'Hiding in the Shadows: The Growth of the Underground Economy', *Economic Issues* 30 (Brussels: International Monetary Fund).

Schor, J.B (1992) *The Overworked American: The Unexpected Decline of Leisure* (New York: Basic Books).

Schroeder, R.F.H., Miyazaki, Y., and Fare, M. (2011) 'Community Currency Research: An Analysis of the Literature', *International Journal of Community Currency Research* 15: 31–41.

Schumacher, E.F. (1973) *Small is Beautiful: A Study of Economics As If People Mattered* (London: Vintage Books).

Shafik, N. (1994) 'Economic Development and Environmental Quality: An Econometric Analysis', *Oxford Economic Papers* 46: 757–73.

Sievers, A.M. (1974) *The Mystical world of Indonesia: Culture and Economic Development in Conflict* (Baltimore, MD: Johns Hopkins University Press).

Simon, J.L., and Kahn, H. (eds) (1984) *The Resourceful Earth: A Response to the Global 2000 Report* (New York: Basil Blackwell).

Simon, J.L. (1981) *The Ultimate Resource* (Princeton, NJ: Princeton University Press).

SIPRI (2012) *Background Paper on SIPRI Military Expenditure Data, 2011* (Stockholm: SIPRI).

Smith, A. (1904 [1776]) *The Wealth of Nations* (London: Methuen).

Stiglitz, J.E., Sen, A., and Fitoussi, J.-P. (2009) *Report by the Commission on the Measurement of Economic Performance and Progress*, www.stiglitz-se-fitoussi.fr (accessed 15 July 2012).

Studenski, P. (1946) 'Methods of Estimating National Income in Russia', in NBER, *Studies in Income and Wealth* (New York: National Bureau of Economic Research).

Summers, R., and Heston, A. (1991) 'The Penn World Table (Mark 5): An Expanded Set of International Comparisons, 1950–1988', *Quarterly Journal of Economics* 106(2): 327–68.

Toynbee, A. (1884) *Lectures on the Industrial Revolution of the Eighteenth Century in England* (London: Rivingstons).

Treml, V. (1988) 'Perestroika and Soviet Statistics', in *The Impact of Gorbachev's Policies on Soviet Economic Statistics*, report from the conference sponsored by the CIA's Office of Soviet Analysis, pp. 51–68.

Twight, C. (1990) 'Department of Defense Attempts to Close Military Bases: The Political Economy of Congressional Resistance', in R. Higgs (ed.), *Arms, Politics and the Economy: Historical and Contemporary Perspectives* (New York: Holmes & Meyer), pp. 236–80.

UN et al. (1993) *System of National Accounts 1993* (Brussels/Luxembourg, New York, Paris, Washington DC: UN, World Bank, International Monetary Fund, European Commission, OECD).

UN et al. (2008) *System of National Accounts 2008* (Brussels/Luxembourg, New York, Paris, Washington DC: UN, World Bank, International Monetary Fund, European Commission, OECD).

UNDP (1990) *Human Development Report 1990* (New York: Oxford University Press).

UNDP (1994) *Human Development Report 1994* (New York: Oxford University Press).

Ura, K., Alkire, S., and Zangmo, T. (2011) *GNH and GNH Index* (Thimpu: Centre for Bhutan Studies).

US Department of Commerce (2000) 'GDP: One of the Great Inventions of the 20th Century', *Survey of Current Business*, January: 6–14.

Victor, P. (2008) *Managing without Growth: Slower by Design, Not Disaster* (Northampton, MA: Edward Elgar).

Wasshausen, D., and Moulton, B.R. (2006) 'The Role of Hedonic Methods in Measuring Real GDP in the United States', paper presented at the 31st CEIES Seminar, 'Are We Measuring Productivity Correctly?', organized by Eurostat, Rome, 12–13 October.

White, A. (2007) 'A Global Projection of Subjective Well-being: A Challenge To Positive Psychology?', *Psychtalk* 56: 17–20.

Wilson, D., and Purushuthaman, R. (2003) 'Dreaming with BRICs: The Path to 2050', *Global Economics Paper* no. 99 (New York: Goldman Sachs).

World Bank (1978) *World Development Report* (Washington, DC: World Bank).

World Bank (1994) *World Development Report* (Oxford: Oxford University Press).

World Bank (2006) *Where is the Wealth of Nations? Measuring Capital for the 21st Century* (Washington, DC: World Bank).

World Commission on Environment and Development (1987) *Our Common Future* (Oxford: Oxford University Press).

Wyckoff, A.W. (1995) 'The Impact of Computer Prices on International Comparisons of Labour Productivity', *Economics of Innovation and New Technology* 3(3–4): 277–93.

Yasuba, Y. (1991) 'Japan's Post-war Growth in Historical Perspective', *Japan Forum* 3 (April): 57–70.

Index